THE LAW IN BRIEF

In the same series

Divorce
First Time Buyer: First Time Seller

Uniform with this book

THE
LAW IN
BRIEF

Michael Heneker

RIGHT WAY

Typeset in 11 pt Times by Letterpart Ltd., Reigate, Surrey.
Printed and bound in Great Britain by Cox & Wyman Ltd., Reading, Berkshire.

The *Right Way* series is published by Elliot Right Way Books, Brighton Road, Lower Kingswood, Tadworth, Surrey, KT20 6TD, U.K. For information about our company and the other books we publish, visit our website at www.right-way.co.uk

CONTENTS

CHAPTER   PAGE

		PAGE
	Preface	7
1.	Origin of Law	9
2.	Origins and Sources of English Law	14
3.	Milestones	28
4.	Theory of Law	35
5.	Constitutional Law	39
6.	Jargon, Complication and Fiction	49
7.	Documents	56
8.	It Does Not Apply to Me	60
9.	Criminal Law	63
10.	Contract Law	70
11.	Land Law	81
12.	Tort	86
13.	Family Law	93
14.	Planning Law	100
15.	Company and Commercial Law	104
16.	Managing Property and Inheritance	110
17.	Intellectual Property	118
18.	Court Procedure	122
19.	Legal Aid	130
20.	Solicitors and Barristers	133
21.	Laws of Foreign Countries	137
22.	International Law	142
23.	Trends	148
	Glossary	152
	Index	158

ACKNOWLEDGEMENTS

I would like to thank Mr Geoffrey Chapman for his invaluable assistance and also Mrs Patricia Watts and Mr David Foster for their helpful comments.

DEDICATION

For Julia.

PREFACE

The public has a general perception of law as being very complicated and lawyers as being aloof and expensive. Shakespeare had some harsh words for lawyers. His character Dick the Butcher in *King Henry VI, Part 2* says, "The first thing we do, let's kill all the lawyers." In *Bleak House*, Charles Dickens highlighted the law's interminable delays in the case of Jarndyce v Jarndyce and a German proverb says, "Doctors purge the body, preachers the conscience and lawyers the purse."

Enormous amounts have been written about law. The Law Society Library in Chancery Lane, London, for instance, is a very large room with the walls covered in books from floor to ceiling. This book can only scratch the surface. Its purpose is to demystify the law and show that, although it can indeed be complicated at times, the principles behind it are simple and can be readily understood by everyone. All professions have their jargon and this helps to preserve the mystique. However, people are generally suspicious of things that they do not understand and so, if some of the mystery can be torn away, it can only do good.

I heard recently of a London firm of solicitors who had appointed someone, a qualified lawyer I think, to explain things to clients, presumably in user-friendly language. What an admission! It should be a lawyer's job to explain a matter in an intelligible way in the first place, without having to call in an interpreter to help.

Although lawyers have had a bad press, when people are asked what they think of their own lawyer it is perhaps surprising how often they are complimentary, regardless of how they feel about the profession as a whole. As individuals, lawyers are by and large trusted and respected.

Readers should also remember that much, perhaps most, legal work is not concerned with court action. Courts are in the background to decide issues when things go wrong. A good lawyer will try to ensure that, as far as possible, clients are kept out of court. This is not always possible but resorting to a court should be the exception rather than the rule, as it means that the parties have failed to agree.

1

ORIGIN OF LAW

What is the definition of a law? The *Pocket Oxford Dictionary* describes it as a rule established among a community and enjoining or prohibiting certain action. Law as a whole is the system made up of these rules.

Societies very soon find out that rules governing behaviour are needed as otherwise there is anarchy, which is a state of disorder and the absence of any sort of government. The weak go to the wall and the strong do what they want.

A simple example is the rule that we drive on the left side of the road. If we could drive on either side or in the middle, it would not take long for all traffic to grind to a halt and for countless accidents to take place. Ambulances could not even get to any accidents and there would be chaos. Consequently, for the common good, we do drive on the left and are likely to be prosecuted for dangerous driving if we do not. This example also illustrates another important point: namely, that different societies can have differing rules. In continental Europe, their rule is that one drives on the right. We just have to remember that one abides by the rules of the country one is in.

Laws are now written but were there laws in societies that have not left a written record? The inference must be that there were customs, handed down through the generations, which governed human behaviour. There is plenty of evidence of ordered behaviour in the Neolithic or late Stone Age. We can take two examples from the UK. The area around Stonehenge in Wiltshire is full of evidence of sustained human activity over an extended period, starting in the Neolithic era and continuing through the Bronze Age. As far north as Skara Brae in the Orkneys stone houses were built at a time when most buildings in Britain were wooden. These could not have been built and maintained without settled rules as to how people conducted themselves. As we shall see later, contracts can be, and frequently are, oral. There is no magic about the written word although the absence of writing clearly gives rise to the possibility of differences of recollection and is far from ideal. Perhaps in the days before writing, important arrangements such as contracts would have been entered into with witnesses present. We simply do not know.

Did the written record develop because it was needed for commerce and law, or did it develop for other reasons and was then found convenient for commercial transactions? Again, we do not know for certain but if we look at the written record as it developed, it can be seen that commerce and law were at the forefront. To take a European example, the Mycenaean civilisation in and around Mycenae in southern Greece flourished in the later Bronze age, about 1600 to 1200 BC, some hundreds of years before classical Greece. A written language associated with the Mycenaeans and known to archaeologists as "Linear B" was deciphered in the 1950s by an architect called Michael Ventris. The records turned out to be archives and inventories with nothing of any literary merit. In other words they were largely commercial in nature. Linear A, an even earlier script, has yet to be deciphered.

Cuneiform tablets dated to at least 2500 BC have been discovered in Mesopotamia but simpler written records of one sort or another go back to about 5000 BC. Some tablets contain inventories. Others show a record of loans, which are essentially a legal matter. It is more than possible that the wish to record commercial transactions of varying sorts more permanently was the principal force in inventing ways of creating that permanence. The evidence would seem to support the theory that writing was needed by societies primarily to regulate their activities and that literature came along later. Societies that traded with others found that dependence on the purely verbal was unreliable.

There is little new under the sun and fraud was feared in ancient times as much as it is today. In the time of the clay cuneiform tablets referred to in the previous paragraph, an ingenious way of preventing fraud was developed. A contract would first be written on a clay tablet. This would then be placed inside another clay tablet which was hollow like a sleeve, and on this sleeve the contract would be written again. The two parts as a whole would then be sealed. If a dispute arose on the contract, the original could be taken out of its sleeve to make sure that the sleeve had not been tampered with and altered. This was an early example of creating a duplicate copy as a back-up, and shows the sophistication of a system in operation more than 3,000 years ago.

For Western civilisation it is the influence of the Greeks and Romans that is particularly important. We owe the Greeks a debt in many areas, but one is their attitude to law and government. They recognised the importance of involving all walks of life in decision-taking. The Greeks, or more accurately the Athenians, are credited with introducing democracy to their system. Whilst this may not be on exactly the same lines as we recognise the word, they undoubtedly understood the value of discussion and debate.

One man stands out for special mention in the field of law, namely Solon. In the sixth century BC Athens was in danger of a revolt and Solon was called on to provide a solution. He introduced a number of reforms, the intention of which was to improve the position of the poorest class of citizen. They could no longer pledge themselves as security for debt and all who had become slaves because of this were freed. All classes of citizen, even the poorest, were able to take part in government to some extent. Solon also devised a code of law much of which dealt with family matters such as dowries, wills, adultery and marriage. These laws remained in force for over one hundred years. They were inscribed on revolving wooden tablets.

Solon has been referred to as the father of democracy but this is probably going too far. He did, however, take some steps that were of great importance to the future development of democracy.

The Greeks were followed by the Romans. Their influence shaped much of what has happened subsequently not only in Europe but throughout Western civilisation. The Romans were great law makers. The name that is associated most with Roman law is Justinian, who was emperor of the Eastern (Byzantine) Empire from 527–565 AD. He reconquered some of the lost provinces of the Western Empire but that is not what he is remembered for by lawyers. He introduced a comprehensive code of law in which everything of importance was written. The idea that there should be a code to refer to was novel and far thinking. The code covered personal and property rights and duties, just the sort of things that concern us today. In addition, there was a whole body of law about slaves and their rights and duties. The empire relied on slaves. This sounds strange to us now but at least slaves did have rights and were not treated merely as chattels. The ways in which a slave could obtain his freedom were written into the code. This was an advance on the position where the fate of a slave depended on the whim of his or her master.

Many legal systems in continental Europe can trace their origins back to Roman law. English law has developed rather differently as we shall see. Nevertheless, our debt to the Greeks and Romans is enormous. Without their influence, our way of life and how we govern ourselves would be quite different.

2

ORIGINS AND SOURCES OF ENGLISH LAW

The sources are common law, case law, statutes and statutory instruments enacted by Parliament, to which must be added European law. We will take them in turn.

Common Law
This is difficult to define. We do not have a codified system like the one developed by the Romans, or like the French with their Code Napoleon. We have no written constitution like the United States of America. Common law is essentially a body of custom that has built up over centuries. It is more difficult to pinpoint specific items of common law now than it used to be because of the enormous weight of legislation and case law. Much of what was originally common law has now been incorporated into legislation or case law. For example, negligence is constantly the subject of case law but where did the original concept come from? What about the custom that a married woman takes her husband's surname? This is not enshrined in a statute but is generally accepted and would have been regarded as the law of the land until recently and, by many, it still is. However, some women do not now take their husband's surname. Perhaps this is an example of how the common law is still capable of

change and development, which might not be the case in more rigid codified systems.

Various legal minds have produced their definition of common law. Sir Frederick Pollock and Sir William Blackstone, to name two, both use the word "custom". Blackstone, writing in the eighteenth century, referred to general customs covering the whole kingdom, particular customs affecting particular districts and certain particular laws, which by custom are adopted and used by some particular court. Although there are many statutes governing criminal law, much of that has its foundations in common law. It is often not possible to find out exactly where a particular common law rule came from. A considerable amount of our law is therefore based upon assumptions. Much of our case law and statutes are based on a bedrock of common law, where no one can pinpoint the exact origin.

Custom as a source of law is a very ancient idea and can be seen in Roman law. However, as we have seen from the Emperor Justinian, the Romans rather liked setting it all down in the form of a code.

Codifying law is supposed to introduce certainty, but the other side of the same coin is that it can become very rigid. The fact that we have no written code does help law to be more flexible and to adapt to the times. Having said this, we do not want law to be so flexible that no one has the least notion of what is going to happen next. Certainty is important when people wish to decide what to do. If this is not the case, it becomes well nigh impossible to advise people what to do. Law should not change to suit every passing whim. Today's fad may be gone tomorrow. Law should evolve slowly and there is sometimes a conflict between this concept and what is seen as the ever-increasing pace of life. It is generally better for changes in the law to be a little too slow rather than a little too quick.

Case Law

There are County Courts at a local level all over England and Wales, but the High Court is based in the Strand in London close to where it meets Fleet Street. High Court judges decide more important cases and their decisions become part of our law. Not all cases are reported but the significant ones are, and they are published in various sets of law reports. More volumes are produced every year, so gradually taking up more and more shelf and disk space. It is possible to use an unreported case to help you in a particular matter but it is more difficult to get a transcript than to refer to a volume of law reports. Important decisions could, theoretically, escape being reported. There has indeed been the odd instance of a case appearing in the law reports quite some time after it was decided, when it was subsequently realised that it was quite important.

In the seventeenth and eighteenth centuries, law reporting was of a mixed quality. Certain reporters were not noted for their accuracy and some were notorious for their lack of it. Some judges would put little faith in the worst offenders and occasionally a judge refused to allow a report to be quoted to him. A notorious example of a bad reporter was a character called "Espinasse". One judge told counsel who tried to quote him that, "I will not listen to Espinasse or any other ass."

The position is quite different today and has been for very many years. Reporting of cases is generally regarded as being of a high standard and there is little or no risk of a judge casting aspersions on modern cases that are quoted in court. All reporters are qualified barristers. Incidentally, as well as various series of law reports, the reports in *The Times* newspaper can be and are sometimes quoted in court.

Although it is the task of Parliament to pass laws in the form of Acts of Parliament, it is the job of the judges to interpret them. Since Acts of Parliament are supposed to be drafted by learned draftsmen, trained for the job, there should not be much interpretation needed, one would have thought. In fact judges spend a considerable amount of time doing just that. They also interpret and develop the common law, settle disputes involving both questions of law and of fact, and they also administer the criminal law.

It is necessary to distinguish between questions of fact and of law. On questions of fact a judge sifts through all the evidence and comes to a conclusion on the facts but this does not affect the substance of the law. Many cases turn on fact rather than law and these are unlikely to be reported.

However, when one turns to questions of law, how does the judge decide? First let us take an example to illustrate the difference between fact and law. In one famous case, somebody found a snail in a bottle of ginger beer, or at least he said he did. Whether or not there was a snail in the ginger beer is a question of fact. Either there was or there was not. If there was, the next question is whether the snail should have been there and whether the manufacturer was negligent in allowing it to happen. In this case it was decided as a matter of fact that the snail had been there. The judge then went on to decide that, as a matter of law, the manufacturer was liable for damages. In many cases, the facts are not disputed and in our example it was not seriously suggested that the snail was a figment of the imagination. However, the difference between fact and law is important.

To return to the question of how a judge decides questions of law, he or she first listens to arguments put forward by the opposing sides in the dispute. Usually this will be barristers (counsel) or solicitors although litigants can represent themselves and have been known to be successful against a professional. The common denominator is that both sides will claim that they are following earlier decisions. This idea of precedent or the following of earlier decisions is central to the decision of cases. A court is bound by a decision of a higher court so the High Court is bound by the Court of Appeal which in turn is bound by the House of Lords. The decision of a court of equal rank is regarded as highly persuasive and will only be departed from in exceptional circumstances. At one time, the House of Lords regarded itself as bound by its own decisions, meaning that the highest court in the land was locked into any mistake it may have made and could be rescued only by an Act of Parliament. There was a possible way round this called "distinguishing" to which we will come in due course.

You can now see why law reports are so vital. In any dispute, counsel for both sides will delve feverishly for precedents to support their case and quotes from judges. The vast majority of cases are settled before they reach court for a variety of reasons. Perhaps it is becoming too expensive or, as all the facts come out, one side realises that it has only a weak case. Maybe, however, one side finds a case which settles the matter. Lawyers frequently advise on whether a matter is worth pursuing based on previously reported cases. Sometimes a litigant, usually with a long pocket, is prepared to take a chance, which may or may not come off. A person may find himself the subject of a new leading case and gain some notoriety.

What does a case decide? The answer is not always as obvious as it would appear. Sometimes a court may give more than one reason for a decision. Are all the reasons as important as each other? What part of the judgment is the important bit or is everything the judge says of equal importance?

This is often where the skill of the barrister comes in. What needs to be found is the kernel of the case, the essential reason or reasons for the decision, rather than casual or gratuitous opinions of the judge on matters that are not central to the case. The two aspects are given Latin names. The essential reason(s) is the "*Ratio Decidendi*" (the *Ratio*) and other remarks are called "*Obiter Dicta*" (*Dicta*). It is only the *Ratio* that is the binding part of the case whereas *Dicta* may be helpful or even persuasive but are not binding. It is one of the tasks of counsel to convince the judge that matters he finds inconvenient are mere *Dicta*.

There are techniques for trying to get round inconvenient cases. One is to say that a previous case was decided "*per incuriam*". This means that some other relevant case was not referred to and so that earlier case cannot be regarded as good authority. Consequently, the judge is free to disregard the previous case.

A second is to distinguish cases as mentioned earlier. Because no two cases are identical, there are always differences to which one can point. The question is whether the differences are material. Sometimes, there can be some fairly tortuous reasoning in order to distinguish two cases. However, by a campaign of distinguishing, an inconvenient case can sometimes be distinguished out of existence. Apart from the fact that one court is often bound by another, it is kinder to say that this case is different rather than have to admit that an earlier court simply got it wrong.

A High Court hearing will be before a single judge. An appeal goes to the Court of Appeal which will usually consist of three Appeal Court judges. If you have the financial ability to go all the way, there can be a further appeal to the House of Lords where there are likely to be five judges. One might therefore have a total of nine judges looking at the case. If one side wins at first instance and in the Court of Appeal by three to nought and loses in the House of Lords by two to three, that side loses despite having six judges in favour and only three against. However, that is the way that the system can operate.

One area that has been increasing of late is that of Judicial Review, particularly of governmental actions. How much and in what circumstances can the actions of government ministers be reviewed by the courts? This is looked at more in Chapter 5 on Constitutional Law.

Do the characters of different judges make a difference? Theoretically, they expound the law and so one should get the same decision whoever hears a case. In practice, one knows full well that who hears the case can be extremely important. We all have our prejudices and different experiences and, although judges are supposed to be completely objective, it would be surprising if they did not have different approaches at times. One difference can be between judges who are cautious and those who are bold. A cautious judge will follow previous decisions rigidly whereas a bold judge might decide what result he wanted and then find the authority to back it up. An example of the latter was the late Lord Denning who was not afraid to make new law if he thought that justice merited it. Some of his judgments are an object lesson in clarity and dispensing justice.

Judges are often portrayed as crusty but they can have a sense of humour. I remember one case where a witness who dressed very flamboyantly, and looked more than a little dodgy, tried to make a joke. On being asked his name (I have changed this but not the initials for obvious reasons), he replied, "Frank Henry Chapman – FHC – Faith, Hope and Charity." There was a hush in the court at such frivolity and what the judge would think of such behaviour in his court. The judge raised one eyebrow and said, "I thought he was going to say Faith, Hope and Credit." It was a clever and witty remark, which defused what might have been an awkward moment.

Legislation

Parliament can pass acts on any subject it likes and this is quite different from case law. Previous acts can be repealed and previous ideas and concepts abandoned. Theoretically, it is said that an act could prevent a Frenchman smoking in Paris. Nothing so stupid would be done in practice, but it illustrates the theoretical power of Parliament. We will look shortly at the position of European law and what this does to Parliament but, subject to this, there is nothing Parliament cannot do if it thinks it can get away with it politically. The fact that a general election comes along at least once every five years is a powerful factor in keeping Parliament on the straight and narrow. Retrospective legislation is frowned upon since the idea of trying to undo what has already happened is rightly thought to be undemocratic. A good example of this is new taxes. A government will frequently say that it will introduce legislation to tax something you are going to do tomorrow, but it will not bring in a provision to tax what you did yesterday.

There are times in history when we have had more and sometimes when we have had less legislation. One can see this simply by looking at how thick the books for each year are that contain the provisions. In recent years we have contracted a new disease, which I will call "legislationitis". We cannot have enough of it. Year upon year we have large numbers of acts on practically any subject one cares to mention. At one time, it was a question of how thick the volume was each year but now we can never get away with only one volume and there are invariably two, both thick! This clogs up the system, as there is only so much time available and, more often than should be the case, legislation is not thought through fully. We might do well to encourage our members of Parliament to stem the flow.

An act starts life as a bill, in other words, a draft. It goes through various stages in the House of Commons, starting with a formal first reading. There are three readings and report and committee stages. During its passage through the Commons, it can be amended and generally is. The government introduces most bills and its objective is to get them through all the stages with the minimum amendment. Sometimes amendments are needed to cover mistakes or points that nobody had previously anticipated. However, usually the opposition will table amendments to water down the bill's provisions.

After the bill has passed all its stages in the House of Commons, it then goes to the House of Lords where it has to go through all the same stages again. The Lords has limited powers, as we will see in Chapter 5 on Constitutional Law. It is generally regarded, however, as having a very useful amending function. If a bill has been amended, it will need to go back to the Commons, which may or may not accept the amendments. In any battle between the two Houses ultimately the Commons can win. After a bill has completed its passage through both Houses of Parliament it needs the Royal Assent before becoming an act. The Sovereign used to be able to refuse consent and there were some famous battles between the King or Queen and Parliament. We had a civil war between Charles I and Parliament, which was led by Oliver Cromwell, and the King was beheaded in 1649. Nowadays the Royal Assent is purely formal and there is no power to refuse. The Assent denotes the date when the act becomes law.

It is possible for a bill to start in the House of Lords, and then go to the Commons, provided that it goes through both Houses. The order is not vital. It is also possible for any member of Parliament to introduce what is called a private member's bill, that is, one that is not sponsored by the government. Such bills stand little chance of proceeding far but it can enable a member to highlight an issue close to his or her heart even if some people would consider it no more than a bee in the bonnet. In each session of Parliament there is a ballot for private members' bills in the House of Commons. Those members that come in the top few places do have a genuine chance of steering a bill through Parliament. All sorts of organisations lobby members in this lucky position if the members do not already have their own idea of a suitable subject for a bill.

Where do the judges come in? They interpret legislation. There are rules and conventions which judges follow in their interpretation but they do have the scope to put their own interpretation on some provisions.

One convention is thought by some people to be strange. It is that judges do not *generally* look at the debates in Parliament to see if these show what a law was intended to mean. The judges look at the words in the act themselves and not the debates that gave rise to those words. However, this is probably for the best. After all, many bills go through long debate in both Houses of Parliament. How are judges to decide how much importance is to be put on what was said? Is an equal amount of importance to be put on every utterance? It is easier to rely on the precise words themselves and interpret them. The word "generally" was used deliberately above because in 1992 the case of Pepper v Hart decided that judges could look at *Hansard*, the official record of proceedings in Parliament, when interpreting acts. However, they only do so where the words are either ambiguous, obscure or lead to an absurdity and even then only if there is a clear ministerial statement which would solve the dilemma.

Of course most of the wording has an obvious meaning and does not require judicial interpretation. If a case is brought on the interpretation of a part of an act, then it is because there are two genuine opposing views as to what it means.

One area that creates a number of disputes is tax law. The Inland Revenue will argue that circumstances give rise to a tax charge and the taxpayer disagrees. Sometimes when the taxpayer wins one knows it is only a temporary victory and at the next budget, or earlier, the law will be changed to close what is considered by the government to be a loophole.

Statutory Instruments

This is sometimes referred to as delegated legislation. The sheer quantity of delegated law that goes through Parliament every year is not always appreciated. The theory is to ensure that Parliament is not bogged down by what are considered to be relatively minor matters. Acts of Parliament are the primary source of legislation and you will sometimes see the phrase "primary legislation" used. However, acts frequently empower ministers to make regulations or the Privy Council to enact orders in Council or some other rule-making body is given delegated powers.

By and large, the subordinate legislation proposed by these various bodies has to be laid before Parliament and it is possible for objections to be made before the provisions become law. In practice, objections are rare and it all goes through on the nod. We have been living with this for a long time but the quantity of delegated legislation seems to increase year on year rather than reduce.

The simplest example is where an act decrees that it will come into force in stages and delegates the timetable to the relevant minister. Another is, for example, where parish councils have certain powers, and under the Local Government Act the Secretary of State introduced a model code of conduct for members of such councils. There is a danger that a government under pressure of time will try to slip things through by delegated legislation that ought to be the subject of primary legislation and vigilance is always needed. However, all delegated legislation can only be permitted under an act. Statutory instruments quote the act, and the section of the act under which they have been introduced, so it is possible to check that the necessary authority is there.

European Law

European law is a relatively new field because the UK only joined the organisation on 1st January 1973. The European Community started with the European Coal and Steel Community in 1951, followed by the European Economic Treaty and Euratom signed in 1957, the latter two being called the Treaty of Rome. What was originally called the European Economic Community (EEC) became the European Community (EC) and is now the European Union (EU).

The main institutions of the Community or Union are the European Parliament, the Commission, the Council of Ministers and the Court of Justice. There is also a Court of Auditors. The relationship between the Parliament, the Commission and the Council is quite complex, and between them they produce regulations, directives, decisions, recommendations and opinions. The latter two are not binding but the first three are. If a member country does not like, say, a particular directive it can apply for a derogation, which is an agreement that it can opt out. It is most unlikely that this would be agreed on any fundamental issue.

One principle is that if Community law and the law of a member nation are in conflict, then Community law prevails. This is a fundamental point. To take an example, in 1990 there was a case concerning Spanish owners of British trawlers. The Merchant Shipping Act of 1988 prevented the Spanish owners from using British waters. The case was going to take some time to come before the European Court and, in the meantime, the House of Lords was forced to grant an injunction to disapply the Merchant Shipping Act in this instance. This would seem to be contrary to the principle stated above that the British Parliament is sovereign and can do anything.

The EC treaty was designed to establish four freedoms. These are the movement of people, of goods, the freedom to establish oneself in any member country and run companies and offer services, and the freedom to move capital about. The idea is to have a level playing field so that there is no unfair competition. These principles do give rise to problems such as border controls between member countries. For instance, how asylum seekers should be dealt with is not easy to decide. Another problem is that of qualification for offering services and whether a qualification in one member state should be accepted by all members. This is particularly difficult for lawyers because law is not the same in every country, unlike, for instance, dentists, as teeth do not vary between countries.

The encouraging of genuine competition in the Community is one of its fundamental objectives. There must be no unfair agreements and a company which is considered to have a dominant position must not abuse that position.

A new constitution for the EU has been agreed which takes the idea of ever closer union between the members a stage further. All the members must ratify this and some will need to put the proposal to their electorates in a referendum. At the time of writing, the outcome of this is not clear. As will be seen in Chapter 5 on

Constitutional Law, the UK does not have a written constitution.

The founding fathers of the Community had high-minded ideals with the horrors of the Second World War still quite fresh in mind when the first treaty was signed in 1951. How far and how quickly the Community moves towards closer union and integration is a contentious matter beyond the scope of this book.

3

MILESTONES

Our legal system has been evolving for hundreds of years but there are some particularly important times or events.

The Norman Conquest

Everyone knows about the Battle of Hastings in 1066. This is because it changed so much. We had a new king who took the throne by force of arms. Although we have beheaded one king – Charles I – and deposed another – James II – nothing quite like 1066 has happened since then. William I ordered a complete inventory of all assets in the country, which became the Doomsday Book. There is really little relating to our present system that can be directly associated with the period before the conquest. Some would say that the post of Lord Chancellor dates back 1400 years but not even this is fully proven.

There had been local courts before the conquest but William the Conqueror set up the King's Court or *Curia Regis* as it was known. He also appointed judges so he controlled the legal system. The judges travelled the country to dispense justice. Approximately one hundred years later in the second half of the twelfth century, Henry II divided up the country into circuits and the judges visited important towns on a more regular basis.

Magna Carta

King John sealed Magna Carta or the Great Charter in June 1215 at Runnymede. It was not intended as a declaration of great principle. It was to solve the problem of a battle of wills between the King and some of the Barons who considered that the King was abusing his position. There had been fear of civil war and the Charter was a series of concessions to remedy grievances. The King regarded it as a device to get him out of a hole but it had far reaching consequences and was confirmed in revised versions in the reign of Henry III and again by Edward I in 1297.

Most of the original Charter has been repealed but one part that remains is that the law of the land shall be a protection for free men from arbitrary imprisonment, or the seizure of their possessions, or the use of force against them. They are entitled to the lawful judgment of their equals. Also, justice will not be sold, denied or delayed. These have become matters of principle and are quoted to this day.

Another important point is that this was the first time that limitations on the power of the King had been put into writing. In other words it was an acknowledgement that the King was subject to the law in the same way as everyone else and was not above it. Charles I in the seventeenth century thought that he was above the law and ruled by Divine Right, but that led to the Civil War and the King losing his head. Magna Carta was vindicated.

Formation of the Court of Equity
Equity is fairness and, as we have seen, has its echoes back in Greek and Roman times. What happened was that over a long period of time common law became very rigid with a number of unsatisfactory rules. One was that writs starting an action had to be in particular forms and, if you could not fit your case into one of them, then tough luck. Some ways were developed to try to get round this but they were not always satisfactory. Another rule was that the only remedy was damages. If someone

took a part of your land, you wanted it back, not just damages. The Lord Chancellor gradually became someone to whom people appealed if they felt that they had been denied justice. He developed a new court called the Court of Chancery and in it he developed rules of fairness. Since this new court and the older courts existed beside each other you can see that there were bound to be conflicts. In 1616 a case decided that if the two systems clashed, then Equity was to prevail. The two systems are no longer separate as we shall shortly see. On the matter of remedies, the new court could order a contract to be carried out. This is called specific performance. It can also order someone to do or not do something. This is called an injunction. An example is when someone is ordered not to go near another person who he has been beating up or harassing. Domestic violence is most unpleasant and the remedy of an injunction is very valuable.

The reinforcing of this principle of fairness is extremely important to this day. It enables judges to create new remedies for new problems. One problem identified relatively recently was the possibility of a defendant in a case destroying vital evidence so that the case would collapse. It is now possible to ask a court to make an order to search premises and take away documents before they are destroyed. This is called an Anton Piller order after the first case which established this remedy. This area of law has since developed because it was quickly discovered that an order could be carried out in a highhanded manner. Although the defendant must not destroy papers he was entitled to protection from having his premises gutted as if there had been a burglary. This is just one example of equitable principles adapting to present day circumstances. Another is what is called a Mareva injunction, also named after the case that created this remedy. It is the ability for a court to freeze assets, such as a bank account, to prevent a party to a case spiriting away those assets so that they are not available to satisfy a judgment. With the increased international nature of much business it is only too easy for money to be whisked out of the UK at the drop of a hat.

It can be seen that Equity can adapt to changing conditions and is still developing. There are what are called equitable maxims, that is, phrases that summarize the fairness principle. The creating of these new remedies is covered by the maxim "Equity will not suffer a wrong to be without a remedy". Another is "He who comes to Equity must come with clean hands". This means that those who want to rely on Equity must play fair themselves.

Great Reform Bill

Although commonly referred to as a bill this is the Reform Act of 1832. It is the one that swept away rotten and pocket boroughs as Parliamentary constituencies. Prior to this some constituencies might have only a handful of voters and effectively be in the pocket of very few people. One or two were particularly notorious such as Gatton in Surrey.

After 1832, this form of patronage disappeared. Although universal suffrage was some way off, it was still a very important landmark for Parliamentary democracy and the spreading of electoral power more widely.

Unification of the Courts

As mentioned above there were various courts that competed with each other, in particular the courts of common law and of Equity. In the 1870s a completely new structure was introduced so that all the courts were merged into one supreme court. There were different sections or divisions dealing with different types of case, but all divisions could use all the remedies previously used by the different courts. There was also no need to consider which court to use, as there was only one. We are so used to this now that it is difficult to imagine what a difference it made.

Position of Women

It is almost impossible to understand how disadvantaged most women were until late in the nineteenth century and even into the twentieth century. The emancipation of women is certainly a milestone in legal history. Women had few property rights until the late nineteenth century, when a series of Married Women's Property Acts were passed to give women some rights. Women from wealthy families nearly always had their property tied up in Settlement and managed by trustees for them. The idea of women managing their own property would have been laughable.

Women did not gain the vote until the twentieth century and even then it came in two stages. First, only those over 30 got the vote and it was hoped that perhaps many women would not want to admit to being over 30 and would therefore not exercise their new right. With women playing such a significant role in the First World War it became impossible to discriminate any more and they won the same rights as men to vote.

More than half the new entrants to the solicitor's profession are currently women, so we have come a very long way since the start of the twentieth century.

Property Legislation of 1925

There was an enormous upheaval in property law in 1925. Five important Acts of Parliament were passed including the Law of Property Act, the Trustee Act and the Administration of Estates Act. Although there have been many alterations and refinements since then, large parts of those acts remain in force and still form a framework that applies to this day.

Entry to the EEC
This was also a major change because it meant that, after entry, the UK was subject to laws and rules passed outside the country. This has been looked at already in the previous chapter. The significance of it should not be underestimated.

Human Rights Act 1998
The Human Rights Act 1998 came into force in October 2000. What it does broadly is to incorporate the European Convention on Human Rights (ECHR) into our domestic law. The ECHR is a treaty entered into by many nations in Europe. It was ratified by the UK as long ago as 1951 and the convention came into force in September 1953. Unlike many states, the UK did not incorporate the convention into its domestic law because it was thought to be unnecessary. It was felt that our common law already gave us the same rights.

It was eventually decided that the ECHR should be part of domestic law, hence the 1998 Act. What the act does is to create a general requirement that all legislation must be compatible with the convention. It will be interesting to see how much difference the act makes in practice. Legal commentators have taken divergent views on this. There are powers to take a case to the European Court of Human Rights in Strasbourg. However, before this can be done all possible remedies in the UK must be exhausted first.

The rights are quite comprehensive and include such matters as the right to life, prohibition of torture, slavery and forced labour, the right to liberty and to a fair trial. It also includes freedoms such as thought, religion, expression and of assembly and association. There is a right to marry and a prohibition of discrimination. Property rights and rights of education and free elections are also included. There is little, if anything, here that we would recognise as rights that we did not have before the ECHR came into effect. So whether the 1998 Act proves to be a major new step or not remains to be seen.

4

THEORY OF LAW

The legal jargon for the theory of law is Jurisprudence. There is a need for law in order to prevent anarchy but on what should it be based? We have talked about fairness and Equity in the last chapter and most right-minded people would say that this must be an important element. However, not all systems do incorporate this. A thoroughly oppressive system can prevent anarchy whilst at the same time being manifestly unfair.

There have been philosophers down the ages who have discussed many and varied systems of law and government from the Greek, Plato, to Karl Marx in the nineteenth century to name but two. Books and essays are still written on the subject. It is therefore a vast subject. Can one do full justice to it in a few paragraphs? The answer is clearly no. However, it is possible to say that most, if not all, systems fall into one of two broad categories.

In one category, the State is considered supreme with individual citizens subordinate to what is considered to be the overall good of the State. Alternatively, the individual is considered to be the more important, and although laws have to lay down rules of behaviour and conduct, this is done for the good of the individual citizen rather than the State as an entity.

If the State is supreme, it is said that this will protect

the underdog. The State has the power to prevent individual citizens from oppressing their fellows. The problem or danger is that those who think that way are often not those who are in power. The elevation of the State easily becomes a smokescreen for the ambitions of a tyrant. Hitler and Stalin are two twentieth century examples of this from the right and left of the political spectrum respectively. In both their regimes the State was supreme with individual citizens having little or no power. Any dissent was ruthlessly put down. Lord Acton's phrase, that power corrupts and that absolute power corrupts absolutely, has more than a grain of truth about it.

An example of a system where the individual is considered more important, albeit subject to restrictions, is that of the UK. We have the protection of the principles laid down in Magna Carta and of *Habeas Corpus*, which protect us from arbitrary arrest. *Habeas Corpus* means, "produce the body" and allows the judges to release anyone wrongfully imprisoned. Our system also allows individuals and groups to make their voice heard on a wide range of matters. This tradition of consultation means that the taking of decisions can sometimes be delayed for lengthy periods. An example is how long it can take for the precise route of a by-pass to be settled. Wrongful arrest and false imprisonment are very rare in the UK and we tend to take this for granted. Perhaps we should not do so.

There are times when even a benign system takes extraordinary powers. The most obvious case is wartime, when the safety and security of the State is threatened. During the Second World War, wide emergency powers were given to the government, such as the ability to intern enemy aliens. It should also be noted that Parliament can pass such emergency regulations very quickly if needs be. The whole process can be accomplished in a day if necessary but, of course, here lies a danger – namely rushing measures through without proper debate.

Another example is the power to detain suspected terrorists. After the outrage in the United States on September 11th 2001, it is easy to see how society may be more ready than previously to accept restrictions on liberty. This is a measure of authoritarianism creeping into our system. The sort of questions that need to be asked are "Is this absolutely necessary?" and "What safeguards are needed?" Provided these questions are satisfactorily answered then extra powers may be desirable but they should be subject to regular review. Once the Second World War was over, the emergency powers were no longer needed and were repealed.

If a government takes extra powers for a particular reason, then, if those powers are not relinquished when no longer needed, they remain available to a future government, which may have a completely different agenda. No dictator says that he is taking extra powers because he wants to use them for oppression. He claims they are taken for what is sold to the population as bona fide reasons but then subsequently uses them for oppressive ones. Eternal vigilance is necessary and no society, including our own, can assume that we have immunity.

One can see that there is this continual two way pull between what the State considers is necessary to protect its citizens, and allowing individual citizens to do what they want without let or hindrance. The key is whether what is proposed is genuinely for the good of society as a whole, or a means to an end.

Not many people, apart from academics and law students mugging up for exams, are interested in the detail of arcane theories of law. I will quote one example in order to give an idea of the sort of thing that is studied. The Greek philosopher Plato suggested an order for the best form of government. Top of his list was not democracy although the Greeks, or rather the Athenians, are credited by many for inventing the idea. No, Plato thought that the best, at least in theory, was what he called a Philosopher King. This was an all-knowing benevolent person who would know what was best. It sounds like suggesting that God should rule in a secular way as opposed to a religious way. The theory may be fine but in practice, of course, no such person exists. Interestingly, Plato puts democracy third on his list, just above anarchy. So much for philosophic theories.

One area that is of concern to everyone is that of rights. We constantly talk of our rights to this, that and the other, be it a health service, education, welfare benefits or basic human rights. This is perfectly proper, and rights are and should remain a cornerstone of our legal system. There is another side to this coin and it is duties. If someone has a right, then someone else has a corresponding duty to provide it. A simple example is that many people have a right to welfare benefits. These benefits have to come from somewhere. The State has the duty to provide those benefits, you might say. That is true, but the State does not have its own money. It obtains money by taxation from the population at large. Consequently, the duty to provide welfare benefits falls on other members of the community through taxation.

Another simple example is that if there is a public right of way over someone's land such as a footpath, there is a duty on the landowner not to block the right of way or to allow a fierce dog to make it unusable in practice. We should remember our duties to our fellow citizens as well as our rights, and also remind ourselves that our rights are not always painless to others.

5

CONSTITUTIONAL LAW

Many, perhaps most, countries have a written constitution. The most famous is the USA. The United Kingdom does not have one. The reason is largely because of our history. We had a civil war in the seventeenth century and even beheaded our King – Charles I. There was the so-called Glorious Revolution of 1688 when James II was deposed and succeeded by William and Mary but this was bloodless. The UK has not been invaded on a substantial scale since 1066 and we have not suffered a revolution such as the French endured in 1789. Broadly, our system of governing ourselves has been a process of evolution over hundreds of years and the need to write down all our constitutional arrangements in a single document has never seemed necessary.

In a previous chapter, we have looked at milestones in our legal history. Magna Carta is arguably the single most important and, as has been seen, this was basically a constitutional matter. The Civil War finally settled the battle between King and Parliament. Although the crown still retained significant power after the restoration of the monarchy in 1660, Parliament was from then supreme. Will Parliament remain supreme? Since we have no written constitution, none can say yes to this question with any certainty. How much power is there at Westminster and how much in the European Parliament for instance?

What is the balance between the two? Is the balance right? How should this be decided? These are important questions and they have brought a measure of uncertainty into our constitutional arrangements that were not there before the UK entered the European Economic Community by acceding to the Treaty of Rome.

The question that constitutional lawyers habitually ask is, "Where does power reside?" This has been answered traditionally by a doctrine known as the separation of powers. Power was divided three ways between the Legislature (Parliament), Executive (the government) and the Judiciary (judges). The purpose of this is to prevent too much power being concentrated in the same people. There is inevitably some friction between the three but this is necessary.

Parliament consists of the House of Commons and the House of Lords. Parliament passes laws as we have seen. All such laws (Acts of Parliament) need the Royal Assent but this is now a formality. At least once in every five years, the House of Commons is re-elected in a general election at which nearly all adult members of the community have a vote (those in prison do not have a vote, nor do members of the House of Lords).

The government is formed by the party having the largest number of seats after a general election. The government has to be able to rely on a majority of the members of the House of Commons. If one party cannot achieve this on its own, then two parties may have to join together to form a coalition government. This happens rarely in the UK because of the system of 'first past the post' voting in general elections. However, in the latter part of the 1974 to 1979 Parliament, the Labour government needed to rely on the Liberal MPs to remain in office.

If a government loses a vote in the House of Commons on an important issue, it will ask for a vote of confidence. If it loses this, then the Queen will be asked to dissolve Parliament and a general election will be called. When a party has a large majority in the Commons, then the chances of this happening are slight.

The third limb in the Separation of Powers is the judiciary. The judges are independent of the government and Parliament. High Court judges are appointed by the Queen on the advice of the Lord Chancellor. Once appointed, it is very difficult for them to be removed. Occasionally, a High Court judge might retire if scandal about him or her is about to break but this is extremely rare. A resolution has to be passed in both Houses of Parliament to remove a High Court judge and I cannot recall there having been such an occurrence. A High Court judge may be criticised by the media or government but removal from office is unheard of. It may be thought undesirable for a judge to be immune from the consequences of criticism but the independence this gives is crucial.

Any interested person can ask the courts to say if a minister or government official has exceeded his or her powers. There have been a number of cases of a government having to back down because of a decision of the courts. No government likes this to happen, giving rise to tension at times. However, all governments invariably obey court orders and there would undoubtedly be a constitutional crisis if a government ever defied such an order.

The Rule of Law
The phrase "the Rule of Law" is frequently used. What does it mean? It is government according to law but not law that is oppressive or perverse. Dictatorships pass laws that are oppressive and curtail liberty, but the Rule of Law does not apply to them. In a police state, the

law is used as an instrument of oppression. There is the fear of the knock on the door in the middle of the night or of being followed or even of being reported to "the authorities" by people one thought were one's friends.

The Rule of Law means that everyone is subject to the same law, wherever they come from and whatever they have done. The poorest and most disadvantaged members of the community have the same rights as the most exalted. Everyone is presumed innocent of a crime until proved guilty by a properly constituted court of law. The police cannot arbitrarily enter anyone's home. We all have the right to express our views unless they are defamatory or likely to lead to a breach of the peace, and we are all free to follow the religion of our choice without interference. When it comes to breaking the law, even the highest in the land have no privileges. In recent times, former cabinet ministers and a member of the House of Lords have found themselves in prison.

We are so used to these principles in the UK that they seem like second nature. However, this has not all come about by accident and there is no divine law that this will not change. We have to be on our guard all the time. One of the prime duties of Parliament is to make sure that our liberties are not eroded by any government.

Magna Carta which King John agreed in 1215 states in article 39 that free men shall not be outlawed or put in prison or have their property confiscated unless this is done by due process of law which applies to all. These principles have been repeated many times since. The case of John Hampden is another example. He, famously, refused to pay 20 shillings ship money ordered by King Charles I. It was a cause célèbre at the time and a good illustration of the small man refusing to obey an instruction he thought to be unlawful.

The essential point is that we do not have to obey anyone. We can do what we like unless it is unlawful. It has been said that citizens of the UK are not merely free but truculently free. The other side of this coin is that by and large we do obey our laws meticulously. We are sometimes taken aback at how some other nationalities will regard some laws as optional, and we have all heard stories of bribery of government officials in certain countries.

There are, of course, examples of misconduct and worse in the UK and there must be cases where such things are never discovered or not proved. However, in the main the people of the UK retain a particular respect for the law, because, over centuries, it has been fashioned to allow us all to do our own thing unless there is a good reason to the contrary. We instinctively feel that the law is "on our side".

Judicial Review

How does a citizen, in practice, prevent him or herself being oppressed by government? Our sense of justice is such that this does not happen too frequently in practice, thank heaven.

The first and foremost freedom is liberty; that is, not to fear false imprisonment. The writ of *Habeas Corpus* is the bulwark against this. It means "produce the body" and anyone falsely imprisoned can ask the court to release him using this remedy. It is very rarely needed these days but is still there in the background and could be used if necessary.

If a government department or a minister is thought to have broken the law, then the High Court can be asked to decide the issue and this is achieved by Judicial Review. This gives the court a wide brief to watch over the action of government. Judicial Review as exercised today is of fairly recent origin. Up to 30 or 40 years ago, what were called the prerogative orders of *Mandamus*, *Prohibition* and *Certiorari* were used. *Mandamus* was an order to do something, *Prohibition* was an order not to do something and *Certiorari* was an order to bring a decision before the court and amend it. These three orders are now known as Mandatory, Prohibiting and Quashing orders, to try and get away from Latin.

Judicial Review really wraps up the three into one. It is an example of how the work of the court can develop and evolve to meet circumstances and is not decreed by a written constitution.

Natural Justice

This is another concept that has developed. The principal point is the right to be heard before a decision is taken. This covers an enormously wide range of decisions. If people are dismissed from their job without being able to give their side of the story first, this is a breach of natural justice. It is not just decisions of courts of law that are covered by this. It applies equally to all tribunals and bodies that make decisions of a judicial nature. For instance, a doctor must not be struck off without being given the opportunity to have his or her say. This principle is a bulwark against arbitrary decisions. Also if someone is nominally allowed to give his or her side of a story but a tribunal or board has clearly totally ignored this, a court would say that being heard was, in such an instance, clearly a sham. It is also contrary to natural justice to act as a "judge in one's own cause", that is to adjudicate on any case where the adjudicator has some personal interest.

Parliament

This chapter would be incomplete without a few more words on the position of Parliament. This consists of the House of Commons and the House of Lords. As mentioned previously, we elect the House of Commons in a general election, which must be at intervals of not more than five years. The House of Lords is currently unelected and still consists of some hereditary peers although most members are appointed as life peers. The relationship between the two Houses has been a continuing problem for centuries and is all about power.

Originally, the Lords had equal power with the Commons but as the moves took place to increase the number of people who held the vote, so the Commons felt that it had more legitimacy. The Great Reform Bill in 1832 abolishing rotten and pocket boroughs was an example. The Lords, in practice, came to accept what the Commons had passed more and more and so the two Houses rubbed along together during the second half of the nineteenth century.

Matters came to a head when the Lords opposed Lloyd George's budget in 1909. What happened was that Lloyd George threatened to ask the King to create enough new peers, if necessary, to outvote the existing ones. The Lords backed down and their powers were reduced in 1911 so that they could only delay an Act of Parliament for two years. This was reduced to one year in 1950, and a money bill can only be delayed for one month. The power of hereditary peers was further watered down by the ability to appoint life peers. Most hereditary peers have now lost their right to sit in the House of Lords and there is currently a debate on what form a second chamber should take. Should it be elected in whole or in part? Should the remaining hereditary peers who retain a vote lose that right?

It can be seen now in retrospect that the hereditary principle for membership of the Lords was never going to last for ever. In fact there had always been an element that had not been hereditary, namely the Archbishops and Bishops of the Church of England, the lords "spiritual" as opposed to "temporal".

One very important power that the House of Lords retains is to prevent the House of Commons extending its life beyond five years. If the Prime Minister of the day was to be tempted to postpone a general election beyond the five-year period, then the House of Lords could prevent this abuse of power. Let us hope that this power is never put to the test.

Devolution

There has been pressure for devolution of power from Westminster to Scotland and Wales for some time. Northern Ireland had self-rule and its own Prime Minister, until direct rule from Westminster was imposed because of the trouble in that province. There has been a considerable measure of self-rule again from time to time in Northern Ireland but it remains a troubled place.

England and Scotland have had the same monarch since James VI of Scotland became James I of England in 1603. The Act of Union in 1707 made Scotland a United Kingdom with England and Wales, by uniting the English and Scottish Parliaments. It will be remembered that it was only after Bonnie Prince Charlie was defeated at Culloden in 1746 that peace was finally established across the border. The Scots have always had their own legal system. It is not surprising that they have hankered after some measure of self-government.

The Welsh have similar feelings although they and the English have been part of the same kingdom for much longer. The Welsh, of course, have their own language and, like the Scots, have pressed for some measure of self-rule.

Both countries, after holding referendums, do now have their own assemblies at Edinburgh for the Scots and Cardiff for the Welsh. Each country now has its first minister.

What is the effect on the United Kingdom? Will there be pressure for more devolution? I am not sure that anyone can tell at this stage. One proposal has been made, namely that Scotland should elect fewer MPs to Westminster. Their constituencies have been smaller in voting numbers than in England, and the idea is that they should now be the same, which does seem fairer.

Another concern arising from devolution is the so-called West Lothian problem, named after the example given of someone living there to illustrate the point. Due to devolution, the Scottish Parliament decides many issues relating to Scotland, such as education. For England, those issues are decided by the Westminster Parliament and, of course, there are Scottish MPs at Westminster. So one finds that there are issues on which Scotland decides for itself with no role for English MPs but, for England, Scottish MPs can vote on those same issues. The result can be that on a vote relating to England and not affecting Scotland, English MPs can vote one way but, when Scottish MPs are added, the vote could go the other way. Most people would argue that this is manifestly unfair.

The Monarchy
The monarch now has little real power. The Queen is entitled to be consulted by the Prime Minister and may advise and warn but the government makes the decisions. All Acts of Parliament need the Royal Assent but this is now a formality and the monarch has not refused Assent since the days of Queen Anne.

The Queen opens Parliament but her speech is written for her by the government. This happens regardless of which party forms the government. The Queen is therefore above party politics and can represent the nation at all times without having been involved in the day to day business of politics which can be hard hitting and sometimes a bit sordid. The monarchy as an institution represents continuity in a manner that would be difficult to replicate in another way.

6

JARGON, COMPLICATION AND FICTION

All occupations have their own jargon and phraseology. The legal and medical professions are amongst the worst. Some of it has been derived over a long period and is therefore time honoured. Whether it is always necessary is often a matter of opinion. The mere fact that a particular form of wording has been around for a long time does not necessarily mean that it should continue. It is fair to say that we all become used to the familiar and so if law students learn particular words and phrases they will be reluctant to alter this later in their careers. There is inertia to change, particularly when everyone else in the profession is using the same phraseology. However, this does not help non-lawyers who are sometimes bemused by the words and turn of phrase used by members of the legal fraternity.

We deal with the subject of legal documents in a subsequent chapter but we will look at the language used and the obscure subject of legal fictions here. Let us start with the language.

Latin phrases are used frequently. Lawyers do not need to understand Latin as a language or be able to translate it. Phrases have their known meanings and are simply slotted into a sentence at the appropriate moment. We have already come across a number of such phrases.

"*Ratio Decidendi*" and "*Obiter Dictum*" appeared in relation to the way judges decide cases. The "*Curia Regis*", the court set up by William the Conqueror is another and, of course, "*Magna Carta*" is Latin for "great charter". We have also referred to "*Habeas Corpus*" which is designed to protect us from arbitrary arrest. Other Latin words and phrases will appear as we carry on, but the right way to approach this is simply to say that once one has been told the meaning of each it need hold no fears. It is no different from children learning new words as they expand their vocabulary. You can see though, that using Latin is so ancient a tradition that it is extremely difficult to change the habit of hundreds of years. However, there have been some attempts to curb the use of Latin phrases and words, for instance we now say "in private" instead of "*in camera*" and "without notice" instead of "*ex parte*".

Do lawyers introduce new Latin phrases? I would like to be able to say no and that we simply stick with the old. Unfortunately this is not always the case. A Latin phrase recently introduced is "*pro bono*". Lawyers recognise that there is an unmet need for legal services, which is not covered by legal aid, and many carry out work unpaid and this is called *pro bono* work. I cannot begin to understand why we have to use a Latin phrase instead of a description that can be understood by everyone. Attempts have been made to change it but for the time being, *pro bono* it remains.

It is not only Latin that causes problems. There are plenty of other complicated words and phrases. Perhaps it should be mentioned here that every legal system has its own phraseology. For instance, although law in Scotland is the same as in England and Wales in many respects such as taxation by the Inland Revenue, there are many differences. The law relating to land is quite different as an example. Lawyers in England and Wales would not understand much of what happens in Scotland and vice versa. Scottish law uses words very unfamiliar to lawyers south of the border.

What are some examples of complicated wording? I have taken a legal magazine at random and it lists statutory instruments recently enacted. One is called:

Enterprise Act 2002 (Part 8 Designated Enforcers: Criteria for Designation, Designation of Public Bodies as Designated Enforcers and Transitional Provisions) Order 2003.

That, of course, is only the title! Don't ask what the order itself provides.

One area that is almost guaranteed to contain many complications is tax law. A book containing the statutory provisions can be opened at virtually any page to find jargon that would make one look like the character in the picture entitled *The Scream* by Munch. There are reasons for this which I will explain but firstly, here is an example, again taken completely at random:

410. Arrangements for transfer of company to another group or consortium

(1) If, apart from this section, two companies ("the first company" and "the second company") would be treated as members of the same group of companies and –

(a) in an accounting period one of the two companies has trading losses or other amounts eligible for relief from corporation tax which it would, apart from this section, be to surrender by way of group relief; and

(b) arrangements are in existence by virtue of which, at some time during or after the expiry of that accounting period –

(i) the first company or any successor of it would cease to be a member of the same

group of companies as the second company
and could become a member of the same
group of companies as a third company; or

(ii) any person has or could obtain, or any
persons together have or could obtain, control of the first company but not the second;
or

(iii) a third company could begin to carry on the
whole or any part of a trade which, at any
time in that accounting period, is carried on
by the first company and could do so either
as a successor of the first company or as a
successor of another company which is not
a third company but which, at some time
during or after the expiry of that accounting
period, has begun to carry on the whole or
any part of that trade;

then, for the purposes of this Chapter, the first
company shall be treated as not being a member of
the same group of companies as the second company.

What on earth does one make of that? It is slightly unfair
to quote something out of context but, frankly, the above
is a nightmare in anyone's language. Finance Acts in
particular tend to be extremely long and complicated.
There are, as I have said, often good reasons. Take
income tax as an example of something with which we
are all familiar. There are all sorts of income. It may be
earned or come from investments, or it could be a
pension. It may arise in the UK or abroad. It may have
had some tax deducted from it before receipt, or it may
be received gross without any tax deduction. The recipi-
ent may be entitled to the income or may be a trustee for
others. All these circumstances have to be catered for and
it is idle to pretend that this can all be done on the back

of an envelope. Also there is a tax avoidance industry trying to save tax and so finance legislation tends to be peppered with complicated anti-avoidance measures.

The legal publishers Tolleys produce a range of books on various taxes annually. Their book on income tax runs to 1312 pages. Five years ago it was 1060 pages long. Similarly, their inheritance tax book is 599 pages whereas five years ago it was 338 pages. In 1998 a new relief was introduced for capital gains tax called taper relief. There is now a 257 page book on the subject of this one relief. This does show that fiscal legislation is becoming more complicated and increasingly difficult to understand.

Another problem is that Acts of Parliament often start out as ideas for regulating some activity or righting some perceived wrong. It is frequently found that putting an idea into words is not as easy as anticipated because it has to be precise. We all have to know where we stand and politicians do not always realise the problems that they are presenting to parliamentary draftsmen. The same can be true of all legal documents and this will be looked at further in the chapter on that subject. Suffice it to say at this stage that lawyers need certainty and hate vagueness.

The subject of legal fictions is peculiar to the legal profession and has its roots in history. We sometimes pretend that things are so. Why would anyone want to pretend that something is different from what it, in fact, is? The answer is to solve a problem. An example was under the old law of ejectment which was an action to recover possession of land and houses. To get an action up and running one needed a plaintiff and a fictional person called John Doe was invented for this purpose. This is why cases in the old law reports on ejectment are frequently entitled Doe v someone else. There was similarly a Richard Roe who was created when one needed a second person. The fiction was sometimes taken further with Mr Doe being killed off after being created. Some old cases have a title starting Doe d, the "d" standing for deceased. This particular fiction was abolished in 1852. That was the end of John Doe, or so it was thought.

In 2003, copies of J. K. Rowling's fifth Harry Potter book were stolen before publication and an unidentified person tried to sell parts of the book to the media. An injunction was needed to prevent this happening but who was the injunction going to be against? J. K. Rowling's lawyers came up with the novel idea of applying for a John Doe injunction as someone had to be named and the identity of the person they wanted to prevent selling was unknown. This tactic worked. Maybe other lawyers will use it and give old John Doe a new lease of life. This does illustrate that the law has great capacity for finding a solution to a problem and looking back into history if necessary to find that solution.

Another modern use of a fiction is "deeming". Something is deemed to be so even if it is not. For example, capital gains tax is triggered when an asset is sold. So, if an asset is not actually sold but is given away or is handed over to a beneficiary by a trustee there will be no tax. What if the intention is that such an event should give rise to a tax charge? That is easy. The asset is deemed to have been sold and reacquired, so triggering the required tax liability. Deeming can be a most useful device in the hands of the draftsman. You can say something has happened when it has not and define anything by reference to anything else.

Another simple example of "deeming" comes in the Interpretation Act 1978. Section 6 says that in any Act of Parliament, unless there is a clear intention to the contrary, words importing the masculine gender shall include the feminine and vice versa. Also, the singular includes the plural and vice versa. These provisions are also quite frequently put in legal documents of all sorts. Lawyers can easily bring about a sex change or turn a single person into a crowd! The idea of the legal fiction is still, therefore, very much alive and kicking, ready to be used if there is a problem that cannot easily be solved in some other way.

7

DOCUMENTS

Documents are a lawyer's lifeblood. However, documents are frequently not used. It is perfectly possible to enter into a verbal contract; indeed most contracts we enter into are verbal. When you go on a bus journey, you hand over the fare and the bus takes you to your destination. If one is a bit pretentious, one might say that the bus ticket is the document, but not in the normal sense that lawyers would use that word. It is possible for more important and complicated arrangements to be verbal only, and there have been cases of money or other assets held on trust for someone purely verbally. This is not usual because most people want to rely on the written word rather than recollection.

The sale of land must be in writing and an attempt to sell and buy land verbally is not enforceable. This is provided in the Law of Property Act. It is considered that the buying of land and buildings must not be left to recollection that can give rise to all sorts of problems. The most obvious problem is to determine the amount of land involved and an accurate description is vital. In practice, a plan is really essential. However, for other matters, unless there is a statutory provision to that effect, writing is not mandatory.

It is, however, sensible to have some document to govern any substantial contract or other legal arrangement. The question often asked is whether they always have to be so complicated. The answer is no. A cheque is a legal document for example. Technically, a cheque is what is called a Bill of Exchange but in simple terms it is an order to your bank to pay a sum to a third party from your bank account on demand. If a cheque you have received bounces, you can sue the person that signed it for the amount on the cheque.

A promissory note is another simple document that typically might say, "On demand I promise to pay John Doe £1,000 for value received." It may include the address of the giver and receiver and may state a rate of interest payable. If no interest rate is specified it is presumed to be interest free. A promissory note is a very simple form of security for a loan. A mortgage is a more complicated security for a loan.

Some documents can be very complicated. The reason is usually quite simple. It stems from the questions "What if?" and "How?". Let us take an example. You book a holiday. What if your flight is cancelled or delayed? Do you obtain some compensation? If so, how is it to be calculated?

Take another example. You rent a shop and the rent you pay is to be reviewed every five years. How is the new rent to be agreed? Perhaps the parties just meet and agree. What if they do not agree? There has to be a procedure to determine this. How is the procedure to work? Perhaps an independent arbitrator has to be appointed. What if the parties cannot even agree on who this should be? There has to be a mechanism by which the independent arbitrator is chosen.

It is the desire to leave nothing to chance that frequently fuels the length and complexity of documents. Lawyers will therefore tend to follow well worn paths.

This also helps to explain some of the arcane language. Often legal jargon is essential, but sometimes clients will ask whether something can be expressed more simply. The lawyer's caution will frequently cause him to say no. If a form of words has worked in the past, why change it? This natural attitude acts as a brake on newer and perhaps more understandable wording. Why redraft something at the client's expense when one does not have to do so? Also, if one were to try to simplify by redrafting and get it wrong, the client is not going to be too pleased.

Lawyers could sometimes be a little bolder in their attitude but there is a good reason for sticking to the well tested even if it seems obscure. It is, however, necessary to explain things properly and perhaps there is room for improvement here.

Information technology has transformed the drafting and production of documents. Clauses and indeed whole documents can be produced practically at the click of a mouse by computer. Much of the laborious work of drafting, retyping of every fresh draft and then proof reading each has gone. The checking of documents is not nearly such a slog as it once was. Although this is wonderful for productivity and makes life easier in many ways, it does have its downside. Printers produce documents at ever increasing speeds and so the addition of an extra page or two from a library of precedents is the work of seconds. Shall we include this or that? It cannot do any harm to include so put it in. This rather lazy thinking can lead to documents being longer than they need to be.

Lawyers could not manage without computers. One thing they have not achieved, though, is shorter and simpler documentation.

Do documents have to be on paper? We have seen that in ancient Greece, Solon's laws were on wooden tablets, and clay tablets were also used in the Bronze Age. Although paper is nearly always used nowadays, this does not have to be the case. Two examples can be given, one from fiction and the other fact. The fictional example is about the cheque written on the back of a cow in a story by A. P. Herbert. How does one get a cow through the bank clearing system, one might ask?

The factual example is an amazing story dating back to the days of the First World War. A certain William Skinner was lost with HMS *Indefatigable* at the Battle of Jutland in May 1916. His Royal Navy identification disc was recovered from the sea. On one side was the usual name, number, rating and religion of the man to whom it was issued. The other side appeared smooth brass, but after cleaning and when viewed at a particular angle it was clear that there were some engraved words. Through a microscope, these words were quite clear and they were his last will made on February 1st 1916 about four months before his death. The will read:

Feb. 1, 1916. – Everything I possess, and all moneys, property due to me by wills, bank, or any other sources, I bequeath to my darling wife, Alice Maud Skinner. Signed this day, Feb. 1, 1916 HMS Indefatigable, Wm. H. T. Skinner. Witnessed by W. H. Taylor, H. J. Way.

The witnesses had not actually signed the little disc but for a serviceman on active service, the will was valid if in the deceased's handwriting. An affidavit by a relative who knew his writing was filed and the disc was admitted to probate. William Skinner's wife had by this time remarried and was Mrs Ballard, resident in Australia. She did, however, benefit from the estate which had a value of £258, not a fortune but worth considerably more then than it would be today.

So you can see that documents can be on any material. However, although signatures are put on documents that are on paper, those same documents are now usually recorded on computer hard drives and discs.

8

IT DOES NOT APPLY TO ME

Many people think that the law does not affect them greatly. Most of us have an interest in famous criminal trials, particularly murders, but we are observers only. There is a perception that the law is largely concerned with criminal matters. We rarely become involved. Perhaps we are summoned to sit on a jury or find ourselves charged with some relatively minor motoring offence, but that is as close as we come, although we may find ourselves the victim of crime such as burglary. Does the law concern itself mainly with criminal trials and the police? No it does not. It is partly about these things, of course, but most legal matters have nothing to do with crime and are entirely civil. We will be looking at criminal law because a book such as this would not be complete without it, but to think that this is the main preoccupation of the legal system would give a very distorted picture.

There are areas of law that we all come across frequently and which affect us closely although we may not realise it. We will look at a number of them and see how they govern much of what we do. They may seem boring at first sight, but when one appreciates how much they affect our lives it becomes clear that they are anything but boring.

Contract law concerns us every day. There cannot be a

day when one does not enter into a contract even if it is only buying a bar of chocolate or a pint of milk or taking a bus ride. We are concerned sometimes with consumer disputes, which are another aspect of contract. Even insurance, which most would think particularly boring, affects us all the time. We need motor cover and house and contents cover or we may find ourselves very embarrassed if we suffer loss. Employment law is a further branch of contract law that affects very many people.

How about wills? One certainty, apart from taxes, is death. We all die eventually and not many people in the UK die totally destitute so this is something that should be of concern to everyone.

Other examples are land law, of interest to all who own houses, family law to include divorce and custody of children, and tax law. Most of us pay income tax and everyone, including children with their pocket money, pays VAT.

First we must examine the different standard of proof required to secure a conviction in a criminal matter and to win a civil case. In criminal matters, the defendant has to be found guilty beyond reasonable doubt. This does not mean that the jury who decides knows absolutely for certain that the accused committed the crime. The members of the jury would have to have witnessed the crime with their own eyes for this. It does mean that if they have a lingering doubt they must acquit, even though they consider that the accused quite likely did commit the crime.

In a civil case the standard of proof is different. If the person bringing the action can prove his case on the balance of probabilities, then that is good enough. It can be seen that the standard of proof needed in a criminal case is higher than for a civil case. The reason is to try to ensure that an innocent person is not convicted of a crime. There may still be miscarriages of justice in criminal matters but it is easier for the guilty to be acquitted than for the innocent to be convicted.

So now we will have a look at some different areas of law, starting with criminal law.

9

CRIMINAL LAW

"Here comes the law" means the police to many people. Criminal law is, of course, a matter of extreme importance but the police are only law enforcement officers. They have certain powers that are not available to other citizens but are subject to the law in the same way as everyone else.

The vast majority of criminal cases are dealt with by magistrates at a local level and only a small percentage go to a higher court. Magistrates are nearly all lay people, that is, people who have not been legally trained. Those appointed magistrates are given training and also have to attend courses to keep them up to date after they have been appointed. They are assisted by a clerk who is legally qualified and can advise them on legal matters. Magistrates must live in or near to the area for which they are appointed and this reinforces the local nature of appointments although the process is controlled by the Department for Constitutional Affairs (formerly the Lord Chancellor's Department). The magistrates make the decision in each case and also decide the sentence for those found guilty but the clerk will have advised them on points of law if necessary. Magistrates have various sentencing powers. They can give prison sentences, but normally subject to a maximum of six months. If they feel that a particular offence may deserve a sentence that is outside their powers, they can refer the case to the Crown Court for sentencing.

When young people under the age of 18 are charged with an offence, they appear before a special youth court where the procedure is less formal. The system works well although uniformity in sentencing over the country as a whole is not easy to achieve.

In some parts of the country there are what are called stipendiary magistrates. They are legally qualified and do not therefore need the assistance of a qualified clerk. They are paid a salary. In London they are called Metropolitan Stipendiary Magistrates.

More serious offences are tried with a judge and a jury of twelve citizens. The jury makes the decision on guilt or innocence after hearing witnesses and arguments from the prosecution and the defence, and instruction from the judge who sums up at the end. Judges prefer unanimous verdicts but, as will be seen in Chapter 18 on court procedure, majority verdicts are possible. It is the judge who decides on matters of law.

We have seen in the previous chapter that the jury must be satisfied of a defendant's guilt "beyond reasonable doubt" and that this standard of proof is higher than in civil matters. A vital question is what constitutes a crime? It is fair to say that for the most part, you know it when you see it. Murder, burglary, theft and assault are obvious examples as are certain sexual offences.

As well as the act of carrying out the crime, such as taking something belonging to someone else, there has to be something else namely the requisite state of mind. This is given the Latin phrase "*Mens Rea*". Much has been written about this phrase but if we say that it has to be established that the accused had a criminal intent, that is a reasonably good approximation of its meaning. A good example of this comes from a case on assault hundreds of years ago. Assault is putting someone in fear that he is going to be attacked or injured. There is no necessity for there to be actual physical contact. That is called a battery, hence the old phrase "assault and battery". In this particular case the defendant was very menacing towards his victim with his hand on his sword. He said, "If it were not assize time, I would run you through." He got off because, since it *was* assize time, it was clear that he was not going to attack his victim. He did not have the necessary guilty intent and so was not convicted of assault.

However, recklessness can be a sufficient intent. For example, if a car driver is totally reckless, such as deliberately racing through a town as fast as he can without any regard for the possible consequences, he cannot escape conviction for perhaps causing death by dangerous driving. He did not start out by saying that he was going to run someone down, so there was no actual intent to kill but total recklessness would be enough.

The crime which excites the public most is murder. This is, put simply, the unlawful killing of someone with "malice aforethought". There must be an intention either to kill or to cause grievous bodily harm. In one case the defendant viciously assaulted an old lady and she died. He maintained that he had not intended to kill her and so should only be guilty of the lesser crime of manslaughter. The fact that the defendant had intended to do serious harm to the old lady was sufficient for it to be murder.

If a defendant intends some harm to a victim but not such as to qualify as grievous bodily harm, then, if death results, the crime is manslaughter. Sometimes, what would otherwise be murder can be reduced to manslaughter by certain mitigating circumstances. The two most common are provocation and diminished responsibility. There have, not surprisingly, been cases when an accused has feigned madness and in these instances it is one task of the court to try to distinguish this from genuine cases of insanity. If the accused is genuinely insane, then the verdict should be not guilty by reason of insanity, rather than guilty of manslaughter.

Suicide used to be a crime until 1961. How did you bring a case against a dead suicide you might ask? You could not, of course, but prosecutions were made for attempted suicide when the attempt failed. It is still a crime to enter into a suicide pact with someone and if death results from a suicide pact, a person still alive after acting in pursuance of a suicide pact is guilty of manslaughter.

There are two types of murder that seem to attract the most attention. The first is the serial killer. Most famous is Jack the Ripper who killed prostitutes in the East End of London in the most appalling way. Nobody was ever convicted and it remains a mystery to this day, perhaps adding to the fascination. There was also Haigh, the acid bath killer, Christie of 10 Rillington Place and the Yorkshire Ripper, to name a few. Christie was a particularly notorious case because a lodger of Christie's, a Mr Evans, was convicted of murdering his wife. The coincidence of having two murderers under the same roof at the same time was too much, particularly when Christie was one of the witnesses at the trial of Evans. I do not think many are now in any doubt that it was Christie who killed Evans's wife and he, Evans, should never have been convicted.

The second type is the nature of the murderer rather than the sort of murder. Doctors accused of killing are an enigma and fascination because their whole training is to preserve life rather than take it. An example is Dr John Bodkin Adams of Eastbourne. He was accused of murdering rich patients and the trial was a cause célèbre. Dr Adams had as his defence counsel a Mr Geoffrey Lawrence QC who became Lord Justice Lawrence, an appeal court judge. The cross examination of witnesses by Mr Lawrence was a masterpiece and the outcome was that Dr Adams was acquitted. He continued to practise medicine in Eastbourne and his patients remained convinced that he had been wrongly accused.

A second example is that of Dr Harold Shipman. He was convicted of killing many of his patients and his motives remain unclear; perhaps it was power. Following his suicide, we will never know exactly how many of his patients were killed by his hand.

A particular growth area in crime is fraud and money laundering. Fraud by its nature tends to be complicated because the offender tries to spin a web of deceit that is going to make it as difficult as possible to find out what has gone on. Money laundering is big business and this now affects all of us. Fraud and drug trafficking, to take two examples, generate huge amounts of money and the perpetrators use many ingenious ploys to try to hide the fact that money has come from criminal activity. All these ploys centre on the attempt to pass money through other people not a party to the criminal activity. The money therefore comes out the other side clean, hence the term "money laundering". This affects the ordinary citizen because, regrettably, too many people cannot be trusted to tell the truth. So, when you open an account with a bank they take great care to check your identity and two separate forms of identity have to be produced. You may also find that, when you deal with solicitors and accountants, they may want to know how you acquired the money to carry out a transaction. "But you have acted for me for years; surely you trust me by now?" you may say. This is fair comment but no stone must be left unturned in the hunt for laundered money. Is this getting to the point where it is an issue of civil liberty? Arguably, it is.

In theft, there must be an intention permanently to deprive a person of property. This means that borrowing something, provided this is genuine and not an excuse thought up later, is not theft. Robbery is theft with violence and is therefore considered particularly serious because it combines an offence against property with an offence against the person. Handling stolen goods is also treated seriously because if there were not people around to do this, it is likely that fewer burglaries and robberies would take place.

Sentencing is a hot potato. Many of the public have strong views on this as also do politicians. Judges hand down sentences and they do not like their discretion being fettered. They prefer to have freedom of action without minimum sentences laid down for this or that crime. They argue that only they will know all the circumstances of each case. This is a debate that is likely to continue.

Sentences that can be imposed range from an absolute discharge at one end of the spectrum through to life imprisonment at the other. Probation orders, community service orders and fines of varying severity are other sentences that can be handed down. Prison sentences can be suspended for a given period of time. If an accused is convicted of more than one offence, he/she is sentenced for each offence. If the sentence for each is prison, then the sentences can either be concurrent, that is they run together, or they can be consecutive which means that they are served one after the other which is far worse.

The main aims of sentencing are:

1. Retribution. This is, as the Mikado says in the Gilbert and Sullivan opera of that name – to let the punishment fit the crime.
2. Rehabilitation or Reformation. The idea is to teach the offender not to repeat the offence.
3. Deterrence. If an offender cannot or will not reform because he wants to, deterrence may work for him and it may also deter others.

4. Protection of Society. The public sometimes needs protection from persistent, often violent, offenders.

Although what constitutes a crime does not change rapidly, it does not stay completely constant. An example of a relatively new crime is causing death by dangerous driving. This was introduced because juries were reluctant to convict motorists of manslaughter, and this is an alternative. Some activities have ceased to be crimes and suicide is one we have seen already. Another is homosexuality provided it is by consenting adults in private. This used to be criminal, and Oscar Wilde was sent to prison for this after a celebrated case. The Wolfenden Report in the 1950s led to a change in the law and the Oscar Wilde case would not, of course, have been brought today.

10

CONTRACT LAW

Every time we buy anything, we enter into a contract. The weekly shop at the supermarket is a contract, as is buying a pair of shoes. So is booking your holiday or buying two seats at the cinema. A holiday abroad may involve the added complication of foreign law, a subject we will look at in a later chapter.

The question that needs to be asked is, what is a contract? It is an agreement between two or more parties and one eminent lawyer defined a contract as a promise or set of promises which the law will enforce. But what are the essential elements?

Firstly there has to be an offer followed by an acceptance of that offer. Clearly, if the acceptance is of something different from the offer, there is no contract. To take a silly example, if you are buying a car for an agreed price, and you then say that you expect various extras to be included in the price there is no contract unless the salesman agrees.

A problem that sometimes presents itself is determining when an offer has been made. Is a statement an offer that can be accepted without further ado or is it merely part of a negotiation or a testing of the water? The latter goes by the name "invitation to treat". This can be an important distinction. A suit is offered in a shop window for £20 instead of £200 by mistake. Can I insist on buying it for £20? The shop has made an offer that I can accept. No it has not. The price in the window is an invitation to treat; I go in and make an offer to buy at £20 which the shop is at liberty to reject. Similarly, adverts are generally invitations to treat.

The other essential ingredient for a valid contract is "consideration". This is usually what the contract is all about. When you buy a bar of chocolate for 80 pence or your house for £200,000, the 80 pence and the £200,000 is the consideration. No contract can be valid without consideration. It is not up to the courts to decide whether the consideration is adequate. They will not intervene in any case where there appears to be inadequate considera-tion but they will do so if there has been no considera-tion. The consideration must have some financial value. In a case as long ago as 1853 a son promised not to bore his father with complaints if the father agreed to let him off a debt. [White v Bluett (1853) 23 LJ Ex 36.] That was held not to be good enough. If the son had said that he would pay his father £1 to let him off the debt, it would probably have been different. A very small consideration might be evidence of duress in entering into a contract, but that is a different matter.

Contracts cover a wide range of activity. The buying of a pair of shoes mentioned above is a contract for goods supplied. Another area is services. The annual service of a car is an example and so is asking your accountant to prepare your tax return. A payment is made for the service. A single contract can be for both goods and services. For instance, a contract is made for supplying and fitting a carpet for an agreed price, which is partly the actual carpet and partly the cost of fitting.

The buying and selling of businesses is another activity covered by contract law. Commercial law can involve contracts worth enormous sums of money but the same basic principles apply. It is a truism to say, however, that the larger the sums involved, the longer the contracts are. Most contracts we enter are either verbal, or perhaps a till slip is the only written evidence. But when one is dealing with large sums, every possibility is thought about and is covered in the documentation.

Some contracts are long lasting. A mortgage is a contract that might go on for twenty five years and we will look more closely at this in a subsequent chapter. Likewise a life assurance policy may go on for a long time. A contract of employment might also last for many years. Although jobs for life are not as common as they used to be, there are still many people who will stay with the same employer for the whole of their working life and this could easily be as long as forty years. We will look a little further into insurance and employment later in the chapter.

Most contracts do not give rise to problems or at least not serious ones. The most common is probably when one gets home after a shopping spree to find that there is something wrong with an item just purchased. Perhaps it is broken or, as happened with me on one occasion, a bar of chocolate had a fly stuck in it! A trip back to the shop invariably solves the problem with profuse apologies and sometimes the offer of something extra as was my experience with the chocolate. I suspect that in my case the object of the exercise was as much to try to placate me, so that I would not report the matter to the local authority on health and safety grounds, as it was to apologise. The till slip is the proof that one purchased at a particular shop. It is therefore good advice not to treat it as wastepaper until one is quite sure that all is in order.

Misrepresentation is one possible problem. The used car salesman saying that a car is a good little runner and that the mileage is genuine should be true but what if it is not? It might be a matter of opinion as to whether a car is or is not a good runner but there can be no doubt of a misrepresentation if it has been clocked.

Another problem can be a mistake. In a leading case in the nineteenth century, a cargo of corn was sold but during the voyage the corn was sold again by the master of the ship for what it would fetch because it had overheated and so, as far as the oreginal purchaser was concerned, no longer existed. It was not suggested that either party was to blame, in the sense that it was known what happened. It was decided by the House of Lords that the buyer did not have to pay for the now non existent goods. [Couturier v Hastie (1856) 5 HLC 673.]

What is the remedy when a breach of contract occurs? This is often solved by a discussion between the parties and we have touched on the solution to minor problems above. More serious breaches are generally dealt with in one of two ways. The first is damages and the second goes by the name of "specific performance". This is simply an order of the court that one of the parties to the contract actually carries it out.

The purpose of damages is to compensate a party to a contract who has suffered because of a breach of that contract. Damages are a monetary recompense. Of course damages cannot put you back exactly where you were or where you should have been. If a holiday is a total disaster you cannot just turn the clock back and rerun the holiday as it should have been. Damages are intended to put the aggrieved party, as near as possible, back into the position he would have been in had the contract been properly performed. This is often a difficult thing to judge. How does one value circumstances in monetary terms? If a case gets to court, the judge has to do the best that he can. One principle is that damages are to compensate a loss. They are not to go further than this and punish the party in breach of contract. Another is that the aggrieved person must, what is called, "mitigate" his damage. To take our holiday example, if a hotel is so dreadful that one cannot be expected to stay, then, if it was supposed to be two star, one cannot just book into the most expensive five star hotel instead for the remainder of the holiday and expect the tour company to pay for it. There has to be a sense of proportion.

A court can order specific performance of a contract. This is a discretionary remedy and there is no absolute right to it. The sort of circumstance where it may be appropriate is a contract for the purchase of a particular house or piece of land. The person buying wants that house or piece of land and not anything else. However, the order must be capable of being enforced so a court would not make such an order where the person selling turned out not to own the land after all.

It is probably true that courts order damages to be paid in the majority of cases rather than specific performance. For most cases where courts are not involved it is likely to be the reverse. Where you have had a repair job carried out badly or incompletely, you do not ask for damages. You ask the person who did the job to come back and do it properly or finish it off. Similarly, I did not ask for damages when I returned my bar of chocolate complete with fly. I wanted and obtained a replacement and the extra bars given to me were a bonus, not instead of damages. We had our kitchen floor re-covered recently. The fitters arrived and were left to get on with it whilst my wife went out. She returned to find the new flooring fitted beautifully but in the wrong colour. We did not want damages but the flooring that had been ordered. In other words, we wanted specific performance of the contract and this is what happened. If a garage does not carry out a car service properly, damages are no good. What is wanted is for the job to be done as intended, so that the car is roadworthy.

Under the common law there is a maxim, inevitably in Latin, which readers may have heard. It is "*caveat emptor*" which translates as "let the buyer beware". This puts the onus on the purchaser to check everything carefully before entering into a contract to buy. There have been a number of statutes that have modified this rule, particularly when one buys from shops and dealers, but for most transactions between ordinary citizens, for instance through small ads, or at car boot sales, *caveat emptor* still applies. Take the example of what looks like an antique on sale at a car boot sale or at an antique shop. If you buy at a high price on the assumption that it is antique you have no redress when it turns out to have been made in Birmingham last year. If it had been offered as an antique, this would have been a misrepresentation, presumably made with the intent to induce you to buy. In these circumstances, it would be possible to claim damages because of the misrepresentation, even if this was innocent. A deliberate misrepresentation is fraudulent and serious consequences can follow. More often than not, if there is doubt, items are sold "as seen" and *caveat emptor* then applies.

It also applies when one buys a house which for most is the largest transaction they will make. This is why it is foolish not to employ a solicitor to check on such things as charges on the property, local land charges and the responsibility for repairing roads or drains. There are a hundred and one things that could affect a property and one cannot be too careful. A seller must answer all questions honestly but is not under an obligation to volunteer, for instance, that there is an ongoing dispute with a neighbour. Neither is a seller under any obligation to reveal that the property is in a poor state of repair. It is up to the buyer to have a survey. "Let the buyer beware" is still a most important principle that we ignore at our peril.

There have been a number of developments, some in recent times, to protect consumers. What these have done is broadly to modify the full rigours of the *caveat emptor* principle. A particular landmark was in the Victorian era, namely the Sale of Goods Act 1893. This act provided amongst other things that goods sold must be of merchantable quality and also must be fit for the purpose for which they were sold. This was a departure from the idea of complete freedom of contract. There is now the Sale of Goods Act 1979 which goes further and there is also the Unfair Contract Terms Act 1977. This, for instance, outlaws some types of exclusion clauses and some such clauses can only be relied upon if they are considered reasonable. A guarantee in a contract cannot be used to remove statutory protection, so a manufacturer's guarantee is in addition to any statutory rights and not instead of them. There are other acts such as the Consumer Protection Act 1987, and EU Directives also have an impact. The climate has changed to give more protection to consumers but the origins of this go back to the end of the nineteenth century and so it is not such a new trend after all.

Insurance

We will now look briefly at insurance. Sometimes considered boring, it can turn out to be far from boring if one does not have adequate insurances. We all have to be covered for third party risk before we can drive on the roads. Driving uninsured is an offence for which one can be convicted in the criminal courts. Although third party cover is all that is required by law most people have comprehensive cover. If the car is of little value, third party, fire and theft may be enough.

House building and contents insurance are also important and if you have a mortgage the lender will insist on buildings cover although he is only interested in the sum lent which may not be the same as the full rebuilding cost. There is a nasty trap which it is easy to fall into. It is called averaging and is designed to discourage policyholders from underinsuring. It is best illustrated by an example.

A house is insured for £100,000 but complete rebuilding would cost £150,000. A fire does damage which costs £75,000 to repair. The policyholder heaves a sigh of relief because he is covered for more than the repair cost and will recover the full £75,000. No, says the insurance company. You are only covered for two thirds of the value of your house and so we will pay only two thirds of the value of your claim namely £50,000. You the policyholder must find the balance of £25,000. The same principle applies to contents cover. Incidentally, it is easy to underinsure by mistake. Many people are surprised at the value of their contents when they go round their houses systematically totting up the value of everything. Also, there is sometimes confusion about the need to cover, on an all risks basis, items one takes out of the house, for instance, watches, cameras and laptop computers.

Holiday insurance is something most of us take out from time to time or even have annual cover. It does not make holiday disasters any more pleasant at the time but at least it helps afterwards.

An insurance policy is a contract between the insurance company and the policyholder. The same general principles apply to these contracts as to any other. However, insurance contracts are different in that they are subject to another principle which is covered by yet another Latin phrase. This is "*Uberrimae Fidei*". This can be translated as – "utmost good faith". What it means is that there is an obligation to inform the insurance company of everything that could be of relevance.

Normally this is covered by the questions asked on the proposal form before taking out cover but these questions must be answered honestly and fully. This is not the end of one's obligations. If an extension is built on a house, the insurance company should be told. If you are involved in an accident whilst driving, the insurance company should be informed even if there is no intention to claim.

Another form of insurance is life cover which can come in various forms. The simplest is called term insurance. A premium is paid to an insurance company to cover a life (not always the person paying the premium) for a given sum insured for an agreed number of years. If the life insured dies, the sum insured is payable, but if the life insured survives the term of the cover, nothing is payable. The premium may be one off or annual. This is the cheapest form of life cover and is a bit like a morbid bet with the insurance company. If the insured dies, the bet is won. People may take out this sort of cover to provide a lump sum for dependants in the event of death. Companies may insure the lives of their key executives so that they have a lump sum to hire someone else in the event of death.

There are other types of life cover which are a form of saving. They will guarantee a certain payment on death or perhaps after a given number of years. These policies come in all sorts of shapes and sizes, and to go into more detail is beyond the scope of this book. Perhaps I could conclude this section by saying that life cover for a large part of the population used to be the way of paying for a funeral. There was a natural fear of not being able to be buried properly and with dignity and a whole life policy covered this. "The man from the Pru" or some other company used to come round regularly to collect the premiums. There is not, for the most part, the same need for this now.

Contracts of Employment

Contracts of employment are extremely important for all employees. There was at one time almost complete freedom of contract and this tended to favour the employer. A person could be sacked or "given their cards" really very easily without much redress. There might be a period of notice, but usually quite short. It was felt that employees needed more protection because they and their families depended on the job of the bread winner.

One change was the introduction of redundancy payments. If someone loses his or her job not because of misconduct but due to the job disappearing, he becomes entitled to a redundancy payment based on his salary, length of service and age. There is no redundancy payment if the person concerned is very close to or over retirement age. The cost of redundancy payments is largely funded by the government out of taxation.

Another change is the concept of unfair dismissal. The idea is to protect employees from capricious employers. There is a large body of law on this subject but broadly an employee can claim damages if he can prove to an employment tribunal that he has been unfairly dismissed. There is no such right until a person has been employed for one year. Many employers will therefore have a policy of reviewing all employees when they have been employed for, say, eleven months. One ploy used by some unscrupulous employers is to make life intolerable for an employee. Perhaps he will be demoted or asked to work in particularly poor conditions. The idea is to force him to give notice and leave, thereby avoiding an unfair dismissal case. This does not work and the tribunals soon decided that this is tantamount to dismissal. It has the name "constructive dismissal". The employee can still bring a claim. Most employers realise that their employees are their best asset and must be looked after decently, but the law does now protect those who do not have enlightened employers.

11

LAND LAW

The law relating to land, and buildings on land, has historically been vital. There are few people that it does not affect. We all live somewhere and buying and selling property, or renting it, is important to most people. Even squatters have rights. They cannot just be turned out of a house, without a court order first being obtained. There is a fundamental distinction in law between land law on the one hand and other property on the other. The former is called "Real Property" or "Realty" and the latter "Personal Property" or "Personalty" although it is no less real.

At one time, in the feudal era, all land was held in a sort of pyramid that could be traced back to the crown. The King granted land to various Dukes, Earls or other noblemen and they in turn would grant land to lesser mortals and so on down the chain. This is, of course, no longer how it works in practice but some of the terminology still has a rather ancient ring to it.

The buying and selling of land and houses is another type of contract which requires an offer and acceptance and consideration like any other and additionally must be in writing. A house is usually "freehold" which in practice means absolutely. To make it more complicated, the full name of a freehold interest is "Estate in fee simple absolute in possession". Theoretically, unless the deeds of a house (now likely to be a computerised record at the Land Registry) say otherwise, the freeholder does not own just the house itself and the surface of the surrounding land. He owns a three dimensional area going up into the sky and down below the ground.

Another type of ownership is "leasehold". In this type, a landlord who is usually the freeholder grants a lease to someone else for a term of years. At the end of the term the property reverts to the landlord. This type of ownership is often used for blocks of flats where it is desirable for there to be some control over how the block is managed and repaired for the common good of all the flat owners. Leases of flats are usually 99 years long, but sometimes longer, with only a very modest ground rent being paid. Owners can get rather concerned as the length of the lease becomes progressively shorter. Are they going to be able to find someone to buy a relatively short lease for an acceptable price? There are statutory provisions that enable leaseholders to buy the freehold in many instances, so this is frequently not so serious a problem as it seems at first sight.

In the previous paragraph the word lease is used to denote a long lease for a term of years which has a value like a freehold house. It is the sort of lease that is bought. Another sort of lease is usually termed a tenancy agreement, and this is where one rents rather than buying. It is a much shorter agreement with a landlord letting to a tenant for possibly as short as six months, but often for a year. Unlike a long lease at a token ground rent, the tenant pays a full market rent, and so the lease or tenancy agreement never has any value in the sense that it can be sold. Indeed, such agreements invariably forbid the tenant from parting with possession.

Historically, there was total freedom of action and two parties could strike any bargain that they liked. Legislation was brought in at different times to give tenants certain statutory rights of possession. For domestic lettings, tenants were given absolute security of tenure in some circumstances. The reasoning was to protect tenants, but what happened in practice was that no landlord was prepared to let and the lettings market dried up. This was changed so that tenants do not now obtain security provided the right procedure is adopted. Those who had security when the law changed did not lose it and there are still tenants who retain their security although with the passage of time their number is diminishing. So, the pendulum has swung back and forth.

Lessees of business premises still frequently have security, so that when their lease comes to an end, they have the right to a new lease. The terms are imposed by the courts if the parties cannot agree between themselves. For agricultural land, tenants also frequently have security with the right to renew their leases when they expire. The reason is that stability for both business and agriculture is regarded as very important. The law has changed so that in recent years there has been a trend back towards allowing people to make their own arrangements and for the law to impose fewer restrictions, but security of tenure for business and agricultural lettings is to a large extent still in place.

Few people can get on the housing ladder by purchasing a property outright. They need a mortgage to enable them to buy. A mortgage is simply a method of borrowing money. The same is true of debentures, loan stocks and other issues that often go under fancy names. The difference between these and borrowing a tenner for a taxi fare is the terms on which the borrowing is made. Obviously the larger the amount lent, the more careful the lender needs to be about the terms. For trivial sums it will be based on trust or possibly a simple IOU. Where the more sophisticated and larger borrowings differ is firstly on when the loan is going to be repaid, secondly on what interest rate is going to be payable on the borrowed money and thirdly the security taken. It is this last point that particularly singles out the mortgage because the borrowing is secured on the property that is being purchased. There is a whole body of law surrounding mortgages, but the cardinal point, which many people know to their cost, is that if they default with their payments, they can be kicked out of the property and it is then sold without their consent. Most mortgages are written so that they could be called in at quite short notice but in practice this does not happen unless there is a fairly serious default.

Titles to properties used to be represented by piles of deeds sometimes with plans that were less than perfect. Increasingly, titles have been registered with the Land Registry and every part of England and Wales is now covered. If any transaction of any sort now takes place for any property which is unregistered, this triggers a first registration. More and more of the country is registered and it will soon become a rarity to have an unregistered title. The Registry guarantees titles and it says much for the standard of conveyancing that there are relatively few occasions when difficult questions are asked when application is made for first registration.

One thing that can cause enormous resentment when houses are bought and sold is misunderstandings over trivial matters. There are rules about what should be left and what can be taken but it is best to agree this in detail. An example is a case when a client moved into a new house to find a few shrubs missing. They should not have been taken but most people probably would not even have noticed. There threatened to be an enormous row over some shrubs worth perhaps £20 with the house having cost over £500,000. It is surprising how often trivial details can mar what would otherwise be a model transaction.

Land can be owned by more than one person. There are two types of joint ownership which have different names. They are called "joint tenancy" and "tenancy in common". Under the first type, the property automatically passes to the survivor on the death of the first. Under the second type it is not automatic and each party can give away his half by will to anyone he likes. If each person leaves his half to the other by will, it might be thought that there is no difference in practice and that both types of joint ownership achieve the same result. This is often not the case and there can be some important differences, not least in the area of taxation. If you own a house jointly with someone else, do you know which type it is and what the consequences might be? If not, you should perhaps check it out to make sure everything is as you want it.

It is possible to acquire land by 'adverse occupation', for twelve years or more. If a person uses someone else's land, without agreement, but the owner allows this to continue for twelve years, then the user can sometimes claim a good title to the land. An example is moving a fence a few metres on to a neighbour's land and hoping the neighbour does not notice or object for twelve years. There have been more blatant examples. In one case, squatters used a house for twelve years. They were then brazen enough to claim ownership and the court agreed with them. This brings us back to the rights of squatters referred to at the start of the chapter.

12

TORT

This strange word means a civil wrong as opposed to a criminal wrong. Some examples are:

- Negligence.
- Trespass.
- Nuisance.
- Defamation.

We normally associate trespass with going on to someone else's land without permission. The well known sign "Trespassers will be prosecuted" does not mean what it says. No one will be prosecuted for a simple act of trespass. It is not a crime that can result in a prosecution. It is therefore an idle threat. Trespass may however give rise to a civil action if the trespass causes damage. This is trespass to land. Attacking someone is a trespass to the person and it is also a crime provided the necessary guilty intent is present. A tort can therefore also be a crime. The criminal aspect may end up in punishment and the civil aspect may end up in the payment of damages.

Nuisance covers such matters as excessive noise or perhaps smoke if a neighbour has continual bonfires that cause pollution.

Defamation is another civil wrong. If it is written, it is called libel and, if spoken, it is slander. To be established, it must be shown that what is complained of lowers the plaintiff in the estimation of ordinary people. This means that the defamation must be published to a third party or parties or if verbal said in the presence of third parties. Writing someone a vicious letter may be extremely nasty but it does not constitute a libel if no one else finds out about it. If the receiver chooses to publicise it, this does not turn it into a libel. If what is said is true, then it is not defamation however distasteful it may be.

Some statements are privileged and cannot be used to found an action for slander. What is said in Parliament is one example. This is why people who think they have been wronged by what is said in Parliament invite the member to repeat what he or she has said outside Parliament. Privilege also attaches to proceedings in court. The reason for this is that, as a matter of public policy, neither Parliament nor the courts should be subject to inhibitions.

Action for defamation can be high profile with both the issue and damages decided by a jury. There have been some notoriously high awards of damages, with at least one case being in seven figures. This invariably leads to an appeal. Whether the level of damages should be decided by a jury or by a judge can be a matter of much debate at the time of high profile cases.

Of the four torts listed above, this leaves negligence which is the most widely known and also the most widely used. It occurs when someone does not exercise sufficient care in what they do. There are three elements to be satisfied:

(i)   A must owe B a duty of care;
(ii) A fails to exercise that duty;
(iii) Damage results to B in consequence.

A surgeon makes a mistake during an operation resulting in some lasting damage to the patient. All three of the above tests have been satisfied. The patient has to prove his case but, as we have seen, this is on the balance of probabilities and not beyond reasonable doubt as in criminal matters.

All of us who drive motor cars have a duty of care to other road users. If we are careless and injure someone, we will be liable to pay damages. This is the reason why it is compulsory to have insurance cover for this risk. We are all guilty of negligent driving from time to time. There is the momentary lapse of concentration, but in most cases it does not result in damage to anyone and so test (iii) above is not satisfied. There can be few drivers who have never said, "I am glad nobody was coming in the opposite direction at that moment."

A duty to someone else goes further than doing something in a negligent way. It may be that failure to do something is negligent. If a farmer fails to maintain fences properly, and animals escape and do damage, there may be a good action against the farmer. A prudent farmer will cover this risk by insurance but, unlike motor cover, it is not compulsory.

A leading case on negligence (already mentioned in Chapter 2 on Origins and Sources of English Law) dates back to 1932 and is called Donoghue v Stevenson. The facts were quite simple. The plaintiff drank a bottle of ginger beer and said that there were the remains of a snail in the bottle. She suffered an illness as a result and brought an action against the manufacturers. It was held that she could succeed in her action because the manufacturer owed a duty of care to whoever drank the ginger beer. The decision was on the question of liability and not the measure of damage. The rumour was that the parties settled the level of damages at £100, worth more then than it would be today, but hardly a fortune even then. If this is true, one might ask whether the case was worth bringing in the first place but it has given lawyers enormous fun since.

Not all damage resulting from a negligent act can be laid at the door of the offending party. Many readers will have heard the ditty that starts "for the want of a nail a shoe was lost", and continues until a kingdom is lost "all through the want of a horse shoe nail". This is an extreme example of an unexpected result stemming from something very minor. One is only liable for the type of damage that is foreseeable. This idea goes under the name of "remoteness of damage". There have been many cases about whether particular circumstances could reasonably have been foreseen or not. One very old case in 1773 concerned someone who threw a firework into a crowded market. Various people tossed it around to protect themselves but it eventually went off and blinded the plaintiff in one eye. It was decided that this chain of events was predictable and it was not arguable that each person handling the firework constituted a new circumstance which let the defendant, Mr Shepherd off the hook. [Scott v Shepherd (1773) 2 W Bl 892.] In another sad little case involving an eye, two boys were messing around with plastic rulers having a sort of mock swordfight and a piece of one "sword" broke off and pierced one of the children's eyes. In this instance, the court decided that this result could not have been foreseen. [Mullin v Richards [1998] 1 All ER 920.]

Although past cases are constantly quoted, there is always the possibility of new duties of care. An example is Repetitive Strain Injury (RSI). This is a relatively new phenomenon and there are a number of different types affecting different parts of the body. The basic concept is injury caused by a repetitive action, probably over an extended period of time. Tension or repeated movement can cause injury. Examples of RSI are excessive amounts of typing and a condition experienced by miners called vibration white finger.

Another new duty of care is post traumatic stress disorder (PTSD) which is an illness brought on by having been involved in a traumatic incident such as the Hillsborough football match disaster or the Zeebrugge ship disaster. PTSD can manifest itself in a number of ways such as depression, nightmares, inability to work and general anxiety. There is evidence that the condition does not only happen after a major disaster and it may be triggered by different forms of incident such as a road accident or a serious assault. Some people take the view that we are heading down the road of too many court actions, and that some of them are contrived and should not have been brought. It is up to the judges to wrestle with this problem as they decide which cases have merit and which ones do not.

The remedy in cases of Tort is usually damages. Clearly in personal injury cases, for example, you cannot undo the injury that has been sustained. As mentioned in the chapter on contract, damages are intended to put you back in the position you would have been in if the breach of duty had not occurred. When money has been paid out for a medical opinion or for a new item such as a bicycle it is easy to quantify the damage. This is called "special damages" and does not usually give rise to a problem. General damages for pain and suffering and to compensate for either temporary or permanent injury is quite another matter. This depends on the severity although clearly a permanent injury is likely to command higher damages than a temporary one. It is impossible to measure this sort of damage precisely in monetary terms. What is a leg or an eye worth? What about someone paralysed from the neck downwards? How can money ever compensate? In many cases it cannot, and the courts have to do the best that they can. It is here that previous cases can help and a sort of tariff built up. In extreme cases, the damages awarded can be up to and more than a million pounds. This might be the position where a young person has been very seriously injured and is going to need much care over what may be a very long time.

There can be other remedies such as an injunction. This is an order of the court and is usually to stop doing something. An example would be an order to stop making an excessive noise where the noise was a nuisance. Damages might be appropriate to compensate for the nuisance that had previously occurred but stopping the nuisance continuing is likely to be equally important.

The basic ideas in Tort are simple, but what sort of practical problems can arise? One is, did the plaintiff volunteer to be put in danger? The Latin name for this is "*volenti non fit injuria*". If you volunteer to be put in danger you can hardly complain when something goes wrong, and this is a good defence to a claim. A sportsman cannot claim if he is injured whilst taking part in his sport, because he knows and accepts the risk he is taking, unless – that is – an opponent is guilty of really reckless behaviour. A stunt performer is in the same position. In one case, the plaintiff went for a flight with a pilot with whom he had been drinking. The plane crashed and the plaintiff was injured. It was decided that he knowingly went on a flight with a drunken pilot and his claim failed. [Morris v Murray [1991] 2QB 6.]

Another problem is if the plaintiff is partly to blame. This is called contributory negligence and is common in motor accidents. The courts are frequently called upon to apportion blame. If the judge decides that the plaintiff is, say, 30 per cent to blame, he will decide what the full damages should be and he will award just 70 per cent of this, knocking off the 30 per cent for the contributory negligence.

There are many cases where liability is not disputed. The issue then turns solely on the amount of damages, or "quantum" as it is called. Is the plaintiff exaggerating the effect of his injury for instance? Where someone has been badly and permanently injured in an accident it is necessary to go into matters such as the expectation of life and how much is going to be needed each year for caring and support.

13

FAMILY LAW

Family law concerns such matters as divorce, separation and property disputes arising from this. It also concerns the vital issue of custody of, and access to, children who are caught up in disputes. The law in this whole area has changed radically over the last forty years or so. A property lawyer dealing with conveyancing or a private client lawyer dealing with wills, trusts, and winding up estates of deceased people forty years ago would naturally see changes today, some significant. The basic structure, however, has not changed. The family lawyer, on the other hand, would find it hard to recognize the modern scene.

Let us take divorce. At one time, this was only possible if one party had been guilty of what was termed a matrimonial offence. These were adultery, desertion and cruelty. A divorce decree was granted on the grounds of one of these so called offences. Many lawyers felt that this encouraged a combative approach and created the wrong sort of atmosphere. Divorce does, by its nature, involve sadness and anger and this cannot be completely avoided however it is dressed up. Property disputes and matters affecting children are bound to involve deep emotions.

It is probably fair to say that having to prove an offence made matters worse than they need have been in many, if not most, instances. Having to prove either cruelty or desertion is most unpleasant and there were cases in which some extremely nasty allegations were made. Also, it was an expensive business and this inevitably put the less well off at a disadvantage. Adultery was the route many people took. This gave rise to the hotel bedroom scenario. The two who were adulterous would book into a hotel and the next morning the maid would bring early morning tea or breakfast in bed and witness who was in the room. The court would draw the necessary conclusion from the fact of who had shared a room together. What had or had not actually happened in the room was not gone into in any detail! When Edward VIII wanted to marry Mrs Simpson, Mr Simpson assisted in providing evidence for a divorce.

The idea of the matrimonial offence has now been swept away and there is only one ground for divorce. This is the irretrievable breakdown of the marriage. The question now is what evidence does one need for proving the irretrievable breakdown? Adultery is one, although it is not now necessary to go through the hotel bedroom type episode to establish this. Unreasonable behaviour is a second, which could be described as a watered down version of the old cruelty. A third is two years' separation with the consent of both parties, a sort of watered down version of the old desertion. After five years' separation one party can apply for a divorce without the consent of the other but there are certain safeguards and the court will not automatically grant such an application. The easiest route is two years' separation with consent by both parties. This can often be done on a DIY basis, although other related matters such as the position regarding children or the carving up of property may not be so easy.

At one time no divorce petition could be brought within

three years of marriage unless there was exceptional cruelty or depravity. This was extremely unpleasant with the nastiest of allegations sometimes being made. Things are different now and divorce proceedings can be started after just one year. People differ in their view as to whether this is too short a time.

All parties are encouraged to go through a procedure to see if reconciliation is possible before a decree is granted. Reconciliation does not happen that often but it is a sensible provision that may cause some people to stop and reflect.

When a judge is satisfied that a marriage has irretrievably broken down, he pronounces what is called a decree "*nisi*". *Nisi* is yet another Latin word and means "unless". The parties will be divorced unless a particular reason crops up as to why the decree should not be made absolute. The decree absolute normally comes along six weeks after the decree nisi. If one of the parties has committed perjury, this would be one reason why a decree would not be made absolute. In practice, it is rare for a decree nisi not to become absolute. It should be pointed out that until decree absolute, the parties are still married and so, if one of them were to marry someone else between nisi and absolute, this would be bigamy.

This conveniently brings us on to two other matters concerning marriage which are comparatively rare. The first is void marriages. The most obvious example is bigamy. I know that the punishment for this is supposed to be two mothers-in-law but, of course, the second "marriage" is void. Another example is that one party is under the age of sixteen since this is the youngest age that one can be lawfully married. A third obvious example is that the parties must be of the opposite sex. Whatever relationship two men or two women can have, or rights they may acquire, it cannot be marriage. This matter has given rise to legal cases where a man who has had a sex change operation wants to marry another man. The law is quite clear on this namely that we retain the sex with which we were born no matter what surgery we might go through. A transsexual therefore retains his/her sex of birth for the purposes of marriage. This also means that a transsexual who was already married is still perfectly legally married to the same person after the sex change unless they decide to divorce. It is likely that the sex change would be held to be unreasonable behaviour for the purposes of a divorce but that is a different matter.

There are some circumstances where a marriage is not actually void but what is called voidable. In other words it does not have to be declared void if the parties wish to keep the marriage. An example of this is non-consummation of the marriage.

The second matter is what is called Judicial Separation. This is a decree under which the parties do not live together and the court can order financial provisions and make rulings about children. The grounds on which one can get a judicial separation are similar to the grounds for divorce but the parties remain married. Apart from deeply held religious reasons, it is difficult to see why anyone would want this and it has sometimes been referred to as a Roman Catholic divorce.

Finance and what happens to the children of a marriage when a divorce goes through are extremely important issues. As regards children, there is, firstly, the question of custody. The person given custody makes the important decisions such as where the children are to be educated or in which religion they are to be raised. The best solution is joint custody so that both parties are involved.

Custody does not include such matters as who feeds and clothes the children and the hundred and one little decisions that have to be taken on a daily basis. This is "care and control". More often than not, this is with the mother but each case has to be decided on its merits. Access is the matter of the person who does not have care and control seeing the children at regular and agreed intervals. This may include days out, weekends and holidays. It is rare for one party to be deprived of all access and this will only happen in the most extreme cases. Readers will know of certain high profile cases where children have been whisked out of the country by one parent, causing enormous anxiety. As children grow older, they begin to decide for themselves what they want to do and the views of older children, although not conclusive, will be considered by a court.

One rule which the courts adopt is that the welfare of children is paramount. When deciding on issues such as the custody of children or access to them, courts will always apply this basic principle. The ultimate remedy is for a child to be made a ward of court. The court can then control the upbringing of the child by directions and orders. Wardship is a relatively rare remedy and is a solution of last resort. However, a child can be made a ward of court very rapidly if the circumstances warrant this. An example is if it is genuinely feared that someone is going to take a child out of the jurisdiction. In such a case there is clearly no time to mess around. It is often thought that the law is slow and ponderous but it can act like greased lightning if the need arises.

Finance has to be settled. Both parties are likely to be worse off financially after a divorce. There will have been one home and afterwards there will usually be a need for two. It is not often that this can be financed without some financial pain somewhere. The court has very wide powers on finance. It can order property to be sold and award maintenance for children and spouses. It can also make lump sum awards by one party to the other. A prerequisite is for both parties to make full disclosure of their means and any concealment will be severely dealt with if this is discovered. Maintenance can be altered if circumstances change such as if the payer loses his job and his income drops dramatically.

The court can alternatively order a clean break financially between the parties. This is not always possible but if the marriage has not been a long one, there is some merit in one party paying a sum to the other, depending on their circumstances and that is the end of the matter. Such an arrangement will not end financial obligations to children.

Humans can raise the most trivial matters and we have touched on this in the chapter on land law. Family law can be a particularly rich source of the trivial causing problems out of all proportion. On the division of property, every teaspoon can be a bone of contention.

"This item came from my Uncle Jim so it is mine."
"No it didn't. It came from my Aunt Agatha so I am entitled to take it."

The fact that the item in question is only worth a tenner does not appear to be relevant. I remember one case where a father was picking up his son for a day out and the arrival time was eleven o'clock. He arrived at ten past and the balloon went up. The mother did not wait even to ask if there had been a minor traffic problem. This was a quite dreadful occurrence and nothing would persuade the mother otherwise. This was in the days before mobile phones but even today it is doubtful if an issue should be made of a mere ten minutes.

Domestic violence is, unfortunately, quite common. The courts have wide powers and an injunction restraining the violence is obviously one remedy. The court can order a person out of the home if an injunction is not sufficient protection. These powers are not confined to married couples and can apply to a much wider class of people such as co-habitees and former co-habitees.

The rules about the division of property between spouses do not apply in the same way between co-habitees. The division of property held jointly when co-habitees separate is, however, something which the courts are called upon to sort out if the parties cannot agree this between them.

The law relating to households containing people who are not married to each other is currently developing. The question is what rights should unmarried couples living together have? Should there be instances where they have the same inheritance tax exemption as gifts between spouses? Can they name each other as next of kin? Does it matter if they are of the same or opposite sex? The current thinking appears to be that for people of the opposite sex, they have the option of marriage not available to two people of the same sex and so any new provisions should be for same sex partners.

14

PLANNING LAW

Planning is a highly specialised field. Most people may feel that it does not affect them and for much of the time this is likely to be true. Then a neighbour wants to put up an extension that you would rather was not built or you want to build one yourself. Planning then becomes rather an important matter.

The modern law is founded on the Town and Country Planning Act 1948. Traditionally, owners of land were free to do what they liked with it. However, public policy demanded that there could not be total carte blanche. There were examples of bad development, such as what was called ribbon development. This was housing stretching along roads like a ribbon without any concern for the surrounding countryside. The planning regime does undoubtedly cut down the freedom of property owners to use their land as they want but there can be few people who would think it a good idea to have a free for all. We live in a small and crowded island and there have to be controls on unbridled development for the public good.

There have been changes since the 1948 act but what it did was to make most forms of development subject to obtaining prior planning permission. This basic idea has not changed. Local authorities control development but this must be done within a framework laid down by government. Counties will have plans and so will local authorities. There are therefore a whole range of policies that apply at any one time. County structure plans and local plans will go through various stages and there will be periods of consultation. Amenity groups such as the Campaign to Protect Rural England and more local groups will make representations in the hope of influencing the final plans, and an inquiry is often part of the procedure. Some limited development is permitted without needing to obtain permission. If there is doubt, a local authority can be asked to give a ruling on whether permission is or is not required.

An application for development is considered by the local authority, usually through its planning committee. It has to consider all material matters and this can cover a wide range of issues such as the effect on the environment, traffic considerations and how neighbours will be affected. Any member of the public has the right to put in representations which can be taken into account. If there is a particularly controversial proposal it will generate much local interest with petitions being sent in and lobbying of members of the planning committee. Plans for large public works such as new or expanded airports or new roads can cause enormous controversy and a public inquiry for such matters is invariably held.

If an application for planning permission is refused, reasons have to be given. This may then allow the applicant to put in a fresh application, taking these reasons into account. There is an appeal procedure following a refusal and this may lead to a public inquiry. At an inquiry a planning inspector will hear evidence from all parties who want to be heard, following which he will make a decision. Quite often an appeal can be dealt with on written submissions only and a public inquiry is usually reserved for larger matters.

The definition of development is not confined to building. It includes the use of land. A change of use requires permission. A change from residential to shop or vice versa is such a change of use as also is a shop to offices. Even changing a shop to a restaurant needs permission.

There are a number of other planning matters that deserve a mention. The first is green belt. Land is designated green belt to protect it against nearly all development and is associated with land around large cities. The land around London is the best known example and the protection of the green belt is a policy that has almost universal approval.

A second is other designations which can be applied to particular areas and for which special rules apply. National Parks such as Dartmoor or the Peak District are one such designation. Another is conservation areas. These are areas that are considered to be worthy of more protection than others. They may be quite small, such as a few houses of a particular character, or they can be larger. For instance, many Cotswold villages will be conservation areas. Yet another is the designation of AONB, short for Area of Outstanding Natural Beauty.

A third planning matter is listed buildings. There are three grades of listing, each having its own rules. The top is grade I listing which will apply to the most important structures such as Clifton Suspension Bridge in Bristol. This is followed by grade II* and then grade II. Most listed buildings are grade II. All listed buildings require listed building consent before any significant work is done but the rules are more stringent for grade II* and grade I. Listing is not confined to houses and buildings in the strict sense which is why I have chosen Clifton Suspension Bridge as an example of grade I listing. Even an old red pre Second World War telephone box has been listed. Also, listing is not confined to old buildings although it is fair to say that the majority are old. A very good example of modern architecture may be listed such as a housing estate in Roehampton built in the 1950s.

A fourth planning matter is enforcement. What happens if development takes place without permission? There is an enforcement procedure which can end with a demand for a structure to be demolished. If no action is taken by the local authority in respect of unauthorised development for four years after the development is completed, then, more often than not, it is then too late to apply enforcement. This is known as the four year rule. Although one would be most unlikely to get away with a substantial development without permission, there have been cases where someone has carried out some building work and kept quiet about it in the hope that no one would notice until it was too late to do anything about it.

A fifth matter is tree preservation orders (TPO). A local authority can put a TPO on any tree or group of trees if it is considered that they should be protected. If a tree with such an order is cut down or even if the owner deliberately damages it, then the offender can be fined and there may be provisions about replanting. If a land owner got wind of the fact that a TPO was about to be imposed, he might cut the tree down before receiving the TPO. Consequently, the procedure is usually for the local authority to impose the order without warning, which it has power to do. The land owner has the right then to challenge the order if he thinks it unreasonable. This is a further example of the planning laws being able to impose a restriction on the freedom of action of a land owner for the good of the community as a whole.

Planning is an area that can arouse great passions. It has spawned the word "nimby", short for "not in my back yard", used in a derogatory way about local objections to schemes that affect people personally.

15

COMPANY AND
COMMERCIAL LAW

How often do most people come into contact with companies? Probably more frequently than they realise. Companies range from the very small family company running the local corner shop to the very largest companies quoted on the stock exchange such as Shell (the full name of which is Shell Transport & Trading Company Plc). All companies are governed by the same basic legislation although many different rules apply to publicly quoted companies.

What is a company? Such an entity did not exist under common law. It is a creature created by statute. The full title is a limited liability company and this gives the clue to its purpose. It is the limited liability aspect that is so important. People running businesses could be personally liable for debts down to their last assets. The concept of a limited company grew up to protect people from losing everything; in the event of a company going 'bust', shareholders normally lose only the money they paid for the shares, which become worthless. If commerce was to flourish there needed to be a vehicle to offer this protection. A company itself is a legal person distinct from the people who run it. It is therefore a rather artificial concept. The company can enter into contracts and own land in its own name. It has what is called a memorandum that sets out its objectives and a set of articles that governs how it is to be run and operated.

There are many provisions relating to how a company can be operated but basically it is run by a board of directors who are answerable to the shareholders. It is the shareholders who own the company. Businesses do not have to be run through a company and many are run by individuals without a company structure or two or more people can form a partnership. The professions have traditionally been run through partnerships and have not been permitted to limit their liability. Each and every partner is responsible for all the debts and liabilities of the partnership down to his or her last penny. It is now possible to form a limited liability partnership although there are strict rules as to how this must be organised. One problem with partnerships is that one large claim against that partnership could be in excess of any insurance cover and ruin all the partners including those who are blameless. This might be one reason for running the business via a limited liability partnership.

There are two main types of company, namely private and public (PLCs). Different rules apply to public companies because of the involvement of members of the public as shareholders. Shares in private companies cannot be bought and sold in the market, and indeed most will have restrictions on the transfer of shares. This is to keep a firm control on who owns the company. With a PLC, it is quite different and generally shares can be bought and sold through a stock exchange. Before a company can be quoted on a stock exchange, it has to satisfy a number of conditions designed to protect the public. In particular it must issue a prospectus, which sets out in detail information about the company and about all the directors and what the company is planning to do. A prospectus can be a long document because it does go into such detail. The principle that the public should not be asked to subscribe for shares with their money, without a full disclosure of information, is a good one.

All companies must have an Annual General Meeting which all shareholders are entitled to attend and for which they must be given proper notice. The small family company can have its AGM round the breakfast table but PLCs will hire a hall and any shareholder is entitled to ask the board questions. Perhaps questions will be raised about the directors' remuneration! For many small companies the directors are the same people as the shareholders but the larger a company becomes the less this is likely to be. In most large quoted companies, the directors will only own a very small percentage of the shares and the lion's share will be owned by institutional shareholders such as insurance companies and pension funds.

How does the average person come into contact with companies? It may be that when, for instance, you have your house or car repaired, you are entering into a contract with a company rather than an individual. It is an individual person to whom you talk and who actually does the work. A company cannot use a spanner or wield a paint brush but the contract is with the company which is a legal person. We looked at legal fictions in an earlier chapter and this is another. We turn an entity which is created purely by paperwork into a person for certain purposes. The logic then goes that if a company fails it has limited liability and this legal person goes into liquidation and then disappears. The directors are a different legal person and so cannot be pursued for the company's debts unless they have agreed to guarantee the debts.

You can see therefore how a company can fail; leaving creditors high and dry and the directors can be walking about without any further responsibility. Indeed directors can and do set up new companies and carry on doing business. This can cause great frustration. An individual can be disqualified by the court from being a director for a certain number of years if his conduct is thought to be sufficiently bad. You might be disadvantaged if the defunct company had given you a guarantee for work done and you were then unable to enforce the guarantee. A circumstance that has affected many people is a holiday company folding suddenly. Holiday makers are abroad and wonder how they are going to get back. Others are just about to depart. Will they be able to go? What happens is going to depend on whether and how quickly a successful rescue operation can be put in place.

When a company, public or private, fails, a liquidator is appointed. This person may try to find a purchaser for the failed company as a whole or for the parts of it that are profitable. If the company cannot be sold as a going concern, there is a sale of everything owned by the company that has any value, down to the last table and chair. The directors of the failed company do not have to sell any of their personal property unless they have guaranteed the company's debts. The creditors are then paid as much of their debts as is covered by the money available, all being paid the same percentage of their debt. Nobody will be paid in full, since by definition, if they could all be paid in full, the company would not be insolvent.

Bankruptcy is the equivalent for individuals as insolvent winding up is for companies. The person appointed to deal with a bankrupt's affairs is called a "trustee in bankruptcy". Someone who is declared bankrupt will obviously not be able to settle all his debts in full and so creditors will be out of pocket to a greater or lesser extent. A bankrupt can in due course apply to be discharged from the bankruptcy. When this happens the slate is wiped clean and there is no longer any legal obligation to pay the balance of the debts that are still outstanding. Whether the former bankrupt feels any moral obligation is entirely another matter. The principle is that no one should be bankrupt for life with no hope of ever leading a normal financial existence again. This is important because, whilst bankrupt, a person is subject to severe restrictions on what he can or cannot do financially. For instance, he cannot obtain credit and so is unable to use credit cards. This is perfectly reasonable, but eventually it is considered fair to give him a second chance.

Quite often, rather than being declared bankrupt, a person in financial trouble will enter into an arrangement with creditors. This has to be carefully monitored by a licensed insolvency practitioner. The advantage for the debtor is that bankruptcy is avoided together with the stigma that goes with it. As far as the creditors are concerned, the arrangement is likely to be structured so that, with luck, they will each eventually recover the whole of their debt rather than just a part which would probably be the outcome of a bankruptcy. Both sides can benefit from this sort of arrangement if it is feasible.

Returning to companies, another area where we come into contact with them, indirectly, is through pension schemes and life assurance policies. Most of us are either in receipt of a pension or hope to retire with one at some time, in addition to the state pension. Pension funds are invested in a wide range of assets such as property, but company shares are likely to form a significant part of any fund's portfolio. When shares do well our pensions will be paid without any difficulty and the better they do, the higher our pensions may be, depending on the terms of the pension scheme. When shares perform badly, pensions are put in jeopardy, so the performance of quoted companies is of interest to most of us, not only to the better-off who may own shares directly in them.

Companies, both private and public, can pay dividends to shareholders, and nearly all public companies do so. A company will increase its dividend if it is doing well and reduce it or pass its dividend completely if it is performing badly. This is the sort of risk one takes if one invests in a company. It is quite different from putting money in a deposit account which should be either completely without risk or nearly so.

Publicly quoted companies can go bust in the same way as private companies. Investors then lose all the money they put into that company but cannot be asked to pay more. There have been some spectacular failures. Perhaps one of the most surprising was Rolls Royce, because the very name was supposed to represent excellence. The name was kept, as it had a value but the original company is no more. Another more recent example is Marconi which had previously been called GEC. It did not quite go bust but investors lost nearly all their outlay. Investing in public companies does involve risk, but if a company performs particularly well the opportunity for profit is considerable.

16

MANAGING PROPERTY AND INHERITANCE

Property has to be managed for people in a number of differing circumstances. Perhaps someone is under the age of eighteen, or has a disability, and is unable to manage his or her own affairs. With the average age of death increasing, there are a correspondingly greater number of people who contract disabilities associated with old age, such as Alzheimer's disease. There are also spendthrifts whose families know that they cannot be given any money to manage. It will soon all be spent.

When someone dies, their assets have to be administered and passed on to whoever inherits. This may be under the terms of a will but what happens when the deceased has not made a will? Inheritance used to be considered a subject only for the wealthy. Most individuals might leave an insurance policy to cover their funeral, plus a few pounds in the bank, some furniture and maybe some racing pigeons or a whippet. Increasingly, people have more property when they die. Now, with so many owning a house, inheritance is not the minority interest that it once was. A modest house plus a bank account can be worth a significant figure. We will come on to this in more detail, but let us look firstly at the managing of property for those who need it, whilst they are still alive.

The simplest way of looking after someone else's

property is by power of attorney. Anyone can appoint someone else to manage all their assets by signing such a power and although at one time it used to be a long and complicated document it is now an extremely simple one. A problem is that it is entirely voluntary and no one can be forced to sign such a document. It is therefore no good for a spendthrift who would be most unlikely to agree to it. Apart from this, although a power appoints one or more other people to manage, the person giving the power ("the donor") can still act. In other words the power appoints others ("the donee(s)") "as well as" and not "instead of" the donor. A simple power is useful if a person is going away and will be out of touch but is not always suitable for long term full management.

A second problem is that a power works on the principle that the donor not only knows but continues to know what he or she has done. So, if a donor loses capacity by some illness or other disability, the power must lapse and cannot continue to be used. If someone becomes mentally disabled then an application needs to be made to the Court of Protection, in a previous era called the Court of Lunacy, for a receiver to be appointed. The receiver then manages all the finances of the person with the mental disability (called "the patient"). This is an expensive and quite complicated procedure. The receiver also has to render annual accounts to the Court of Protection, so the expense is ongoing.

There used to be no way round this difficulty but now there is what is called an enduring power of attorney. This is a type of power in which the donor says that it is to continue to be used even after he/she loses mental capacity. Provided the donor has been fully advised as to the implications before signing, an enduring power cuts out most of the difficulties associated with the Court of Protection. As life expectation increases, so enduring

powers become more common. A donor can put conditions in a power, and limit its scope, if this is desired. The
most frequent is that the power can only be used once the
donor does become incapable and cannot be used before
this. There are safeguards and a particular procedure has
to be gone through, involving the Court of Protection, as
soon as a donor does lose capacity. Who is chosen as the
donee of the power is clearly crucial.

Powers of attorney work where the donor agrees what
is to be done. Another solution is needed for those who
will not agree, such as the spendthrift referred to above or
to make provision for a disabled person. In these circumstances, assets can often be put into trust. For example, a
parent might put assets into a trust for the benefit of a
child, rather than making an outright gift. Trustees are
appointed to look after the property. There can also be
tax reasons why a trust might be a good idea. There are a
number of trust arrangements that can save significant
amounts of tax.

I remember one extreme case where a beneficiary of a
trust wrote to say that if he was not sent more money, he
would kill himself and had written a letter to this effect
to be handed to the coroner after his death. This was just
the culmination of a long line of threats and turned out
to be an idle one like all the others, after he was asked to
come and discuss it. Another, this time a lady skilled in
spinning yarns, said that she literally had no food in the
house and would starve to death if she was not sent some
money at once.

Another reason for a trust is to ensure that the capital
lands up in the right hands. Money owned absolutely by
someone can be disposed of by him or given away to
anyone either during his lifetime or by his will on death.
So, if you suspect that anything you give to one or more
of your children, for instance, is going to be passed on
eventually to someone of whom you disapprove, an

answer is to put the property in trust with you deciding what is going to happen. There are rules about how long property can be kept in trust because it is against public policy for private individuals to be able to tie property up indefinitely. Putting property in trust for a particular reason is one thing, but trying to keep property in trust for no particular reason is quite another.

Trustees have various powers and duties laid down by the Trustee Act 1925 and subsequent acts. The document setting up the trust can enlarge on this. Trustees are accountable to their beneficiaries and they can be taken to court if they commit a breach of trust that causes loss. Trustees have a high duty of care and the law is keen to ensure that looking after other people's assets is regarded with the importance it deserves.

Most of the above is concerned with private trusts. Charitable trusts are different in a number of ways. Charities are allowed to continue indefinitely unlike private trusts. They also have tax advantages and they are governed by the Charity Commission. Charities need to submit accounts to the Commission annually and the Commission can ask questions. Ultimately, if a charity behaves in a way not compatible with its privileged status and will not mend its ways, there are procedures for removing charitable status.

What exactly is a charity? There is a strict definition and there are three principal areas covered by the definition namely poverty, education and religion. A very important principle is that once property has been given to a charity, it must be used for charitable purposes. It cannot be used for a non-charitable purpose. Sometimes, charitable trustees have to go to the Charity Commission with what is called a scheme if they want to do something that is not specifically authorised by the trust document. The scheme has to be approved before it can be put into effect. If money is collected from the public and the original purpose is not capable of being performed then the money will have to be returned to the subscribers. The safeguards provided by the Charity Commission are important in order to give the public confidence that money they give for charitable purposes is not going to be misused. There have been instances where it has been alleged that too much money has been spent on administration and not enough on good works. The Commission can investigate such allegations. Politics is not a charitable object and any charity that becomes too political in its operation will be warned to mend its ways. It is not a good argument to say that an organisation is partly charitable. To preserve its status, it must be completely charitable in what it does.

We now return to inheritance and wills. First, however, we will look at what is termed a living will. This appears, at first sight, to be a contradiction in terms. Does not a will by definition only come into effect when the maker of it dies? This is true of a traditional will, but a living will is a more recent idea which has been brought about by advances in medical science. People can be kept alive with little or no quality of life in a way that used not to be possible. A living will is an advance declaration of wishes on medical treatment which may be available for various illnesses and conditions. Some people may be fearful of what they may possibly be subjected to in order to keep them alive. In particular there may be a fear of the loss of dignity. A living will is a statement for the benefit of doctors and family. The wording of a living will has to be very carefully drafted. In particular it cannot authorise euthanasia because this is illegal and anyone who assists a person to die is committing a criminal offence. No one should complete a living will without first discussing it with his or her doctor and close family, although there is no legal obligation to do so.

It is surprising how many people fail to make a will

and I am not referring to a living will. Is it considered bad luck or tantamount to signing one's own death warrant? There are some who think they do not need one because what they want will happen anyway. This is unlikely to be the case and what happens to the property of people who die without a will is quite complicated. In particular, if you are living with someone but not married, your partner will not automatically receive anything at all.

As we have seen, in the UK we are all able to do what we want unless this is specifically prohibited by law. This principle applies to wills as much as other things. One is basically free to give away property by will to whom one pleases. In most continental European countries, the law decrees how a proportion of your property will devolve and this can be up to two thirds. Spouses and children have certain absolute rights that cannot be taken away. This shows a very different approach to the issue of inheritance. UK citizens can find themselves caught up in this if they own a house in Spain, France or Italy for instance. We are not used to being told how our assets are to be dealt with on death.

Are there any safeguards for members of the family left out of a will? The answer is yes. UK law does not approach this by dictating set proportions that certain people must have. What it does is to say that although there is still freedom of action, there are certain people to whom the deceased owed obligations and who cannot be entirely ignored. A spouse is an example, as is anyone who was maintained by the deceased before his/her death. Not even children have any automatic right although they may be able to show need. A claim can be made under the Inheritance (Family Provisions) Act. The ability to make a claim is therefore a statutory matter and there is no such right under the common law. A judge is asked to make reasonable provision for someone making a claim and so the court decides the issue. The court may approve a package agreed between the parties without a full hearing. This is a good illustration of the principle of law that everyone should have complete freedom of action unless the law says otherwise, and does mark the common law system as being different from the civil law system practised in most of continental Europe.

Wills need careful drafting, illustrated by one case of a home-made will. The testator simply said "All for mother." This sounds cut and dried but the problem was that the testator referred to his wife as "mother". So who was to benefit, his wife or his mother? The court decided that he meant his wife but it shows how easy it is for there to be ambiguity. As someone with a slightly macabre sense of humour has said, you have to get a will dead right. A codicil is simply an amendment to a will. If someone wants to make some minor changes to his will, there is no need to prepare a completely new will and a codicil is quite adequate. Indeed one can have more than one codicil. The most I have come across is seven codicils as well as the will.

What is probate? The grant of probate is simply a folder saying at the front that probate has been granted in respect of the estate of Joe Bloggs to the executors named in the will. It is dated and the size of the estate is shown. The court's seal is embossed on it. Into this folder is clipped a photocopy of the will and any codicils. The executors obtain probate by going through the correct procedure, including paying inheritance tax where the estate is large enough. The Probate Registry, which is a branch of the High Court, sends out the grant of probate once it is satisfied that the application is in order. If the Registry has any queries, these will have to be answered first.

The granting of probate is therefore a court procedure and, by it, the court is confirming that the will is valid and that the executors are properly appointed to administer the estate. The importance is therefore that it proves the competence of the executors to deal with all the assets. Since probate is issued by the court, ultimate control of executors is exercised by the court. All wills admitted to probate are public documents and anyone can order copies of any such will from the Principal Probate Registry in London for a modest fee. Many people say that they would rather their will was not available for anyone to see, but complete openness, so that there can be no funny business, is part of the system.

A will can be contested. There is a procedure which anyone can initiate which stops probate being granted. Various steps can then be taken by both sides to what has become a dispute and, if this becomes a serious dispute that cannot be resolved, the matter may eventually come before a judge for a decision. A dispute could be about whether the person making the will knew what he was doing or was put under undue pressure. It might be about whether the signature on the will is genuine.

Another kind of dispute is not about whether the will is valid but how to interpret it. The "All for mother" will referred to above is an example. Nobody alleged that the will was invalid but what did it mean? There are probably as many disputes over what the wording of a will actually means as there are on whether it is valid in the first place.

17

INTELLECTUAL PROPERTY

We all own property of some sort even if it is only the clothes we stand up in. Most people will own some furniture and perhaps a motor car or just a push bike. Many own houses and expensive electronic equipment. All these things are tangible, but there is another whole class of property that goes under the name of intellectual property. These are perhaps best described as creative items of property, stemming from the use of the brain rather than objects that one can see and touch. Patents, Trade Marks and Copyright are all types of intellectual property and we will take them in turn.

A patent is a legal way of protecting an invention. If you invent something new, you will want to prevent other people copying it. This is done by registering a patent at the Patent Office. There is a set procedure for registration which may take some time, but putting in the application will preserve the rights of the inventor until the process is complete. One does, of course, have to show that it really is a new idea and not the same as a previously registered patent or something very close to it.

Patent Agents belong to a small profession that specialises in this field and anyone who wishes to register a patent is well advised to get advice, although one can do it oneself. Patents have to be separately registered in other countries and this is a highly specialised area.

Having successfully registered a patent, the inventor can either produce the product himself or license someone else to do it. Often, finding a company with both sufficient financial muscle and the interest to exploit a patent can be very difficult and some patented ideas are never fully exploited. However, if the inventor can get his invention up and running, it can generate a great deal of money either through his own efforts or through licence fees earned.

Next, we turn to trade marks. We are all familiar with many such marks such as BP, ICI, and Ford. Trade marks can be registered so that they cannot be used by anyone else, in a rather similar way to a patent. For instance, if a company produces a product under a distinctive name, it can register that name as a trade mark. We give our dog conditioning tablets called "Vetzyme". This is registered as a trade mark and is stated as such on the packaging. Have a look at the packaging of products that you buy and you will quite frequently see a statement that a particular mark or name is registered as a trade mark.

If the word itself is not sufficiently distinctive, then to be registered, the mark generally needs some other distinctive aspect. For instance, if we take the example of Ford motor cars, the word "Ford" is written in a particular way and it is this that cannot be copied. It does not mean that a Mr Ford who runs the local sweet shop is prevented from using his name on the shop front. Similarly, a word that we all use in ordinary conversation is not likely to be registered unless there is some distinctive element. An example of such a distinction is "Head & Shoulders", which is a registered mark and appears on bottles of shampoo. Marks are registered for particular classes of product and if a registration is for one sort of product it does not automatically cover others.

There is also a limitation on some marks that will be

registered. If something is regarded as obscene, for instance, then it will be refused acceptance. The word "Royal" is also not available just to anyone who thinks it would help his or her business.

People rarely copy a well known mark precisely. This is asking for trouble. A mark can be very valuable and is often fiercely protected. What does sometimes happen is that someone prepares and uses a mark that is similar but not identical to an established one. This is called "passing off". It is pretending to be someone else and trying to obtain a free ride on their reputation. This can give rise to an action for damages and, more importantly, an injunction to prevent the continued use of the offending mark. If a case reaches court, there will be arguments on one side pointing out all the similarities in form and colour and layout and contrary arguments from the other side highlighting all the differences. It should be pointed out that it is still passing off even if it is quite innocent and was not a deliberate attempt to confuse the public. The question is whether the public would be confused.

We now turn to copyright. What is it? It is the right to use what you write as you wish to do. You can stop anyone else using your work unless they have your consent. The mere act of writing something original creates copyright in it. This applies to your shopping list as much as a book. However the question of what the copyright is worth is quite another matter. Your shopping list clearly has no commercial value whatever. Copyright applies not only to books but also to music, art and computer programs. Some literary works may also have valuable film or television rights.

It is possible to publish your works yourself but it is more usual to find a publisher to do it for you or one can use a literary agent, for a consideration of course. There have been some notable authors who have had to go down the self publication route because they could not find a publisher to take their work. Beatrix Potter started in this way.

What an author frequently does is to enter into a contract with a publisher which gives that author royalties on every book sold, so the more that are sold, the more the author receives. Alternatively, an author may sell his work for a fixed fee, regardless of how many books are sold. Copyright used to last for the life of the author plus fifty years. This has been increased to life plus seventy years.

An author has to beware of plagiarism. In other words he or she must not copy other work protected by copyright. It is in order to copy a small number of words. This can give rise to arguments as to whether the copying has gone too far or not. One can always get round this by asking for permission to use extracts from another book provided there is an acknowledgment of this.

Another possible problem is libel. If a book contains derogatory remarks about someone it may give rise to a libel action, particularly if characters are drawn from life as they frequently are. The author may be advised to change the name and background and even the sex of a character so that there is less likelihood of someone claiming to be libelled.

For particularly famous books or plays, royalties can be extremely high. Since copyright continues for many years after the author dies, it may have a substantial value not only during lifetime but on death as well. This may cause tax problems beyond the scope of this book. An author can and should make a will and in it he or she is able to leave royalties earned after death to anyone. It is usually members of the author's family who benefit, but it could be a charity. One particularly celebrated example of a charitable gift was the late J. M. Barrie who left the royalties on *Peter Pan* to what is now called The Great Ormond Street Hospital Children's Charity.

18

COURT PROCEDURE

What is the purpose of courts? The answer is that they are to settle disputes. They are not designed specifically to make law. The High Court, the Court of Appeal and the House of Lords may make law as part of the process of deciding a dispute but the settling of the dispute is their primary function. The majority of civil cases are decided in the County Courts, which are in most major centres of population. It is only a small fraction that reaches the High Court. The procedure in the County Court is simpler and quicker than in the High Court. County Courts have jurisdiction up to a certain level, above which a case usually has to go to the High Court.

Small Claims Courts are part of the County Court system. Their purpose is to deal with small claims in a simple way and they are less formal than County Courts. The idea is to enable people to settle modest disputes quickly, and without incurring legal fees. Small Claims Courts can currently hear cases involving sums of up to £5,000, which for many is not a small amount. Some cases are not suitable for the Small Claims Court, for instance, if a difficult point of law is involved.

Criminal courts are not different from civil courts in that they also have an issue to decide. The issue or dispute is whether the accused person is guilty or innocent. There are two sides namely the prosecution, usually by the crown, (although private prosecutions are possible) and the defence. Each side will be represented by a lawyer in all serious cases. Both sides will present their case with witnesses and then the lawyers will make closing speeches. Magistrates will then make their decision with the help of their legally qualified clerk. In more serious cases before a judge in the Crown Court, he will sum up for the benefit of the jury before they go to the jury room to discuss and reach a decision as to guilt or innocence. If they want guidance from the judge, they can always ask for it. Judges prefer unanimous jury decisions but a majority of 11 to 1 or 10 to 2 will suffice. After the verdict the defendant is either released or sentenced.

Civil cases will have a dispute to settle and, again, all parties are entitled to be represented by lawyers although it is perfectly possible for a litigant to appear in person unrepresented. Judges are invariably helpful to litigants who appear unrepresented and guide them through the procedures. Litigants sometimes win cases even when faced by experienced barristers.

As has already been seen, cases can be decided on fact or law. Either or both may determine the result of a case. Juries are relatively uncommon in civil cases. They are used for defamation and there have been instances of juries awarding spectacular damages in some cases. Judges, on appeal, tend to award lower figures in defamation cases and there has been debate about whether juries are the right body to decide the amount of damages in such instances. It is, however, the judges who decide most civil actions.

A hearing in court is the culmination of a dispute and much happens before the dispute comes to court. In fact, the majority of cases are settled before a hearing and settlement can take place from a very early stage right up to the door of the court. A case starts with a summons, or a claim form which used to be called a writ, which sets out what the person bringing the case thinks is the wrong and what he/she is entitled to. The initial document has to contain enough to show what it is all about but will not go into the minutiae.

There then follows a series of document exchanges designed progressively to discover all the facts and refine the issues. They go by various names such as a defence, and disclosure and inspection of documents. The purpose of disclosure and inspection is to ascertain that the various documents, that will have been referred to, do actually exist and do say what it has been alleged that they say. The documents that are batted back and forth are called "the pleadings" or "statements of case" and the point at which this process ends is sometimes referred to as the close of pleadings. It is usually a point at which to take stock and decide whether one really has a strong case or not. If not, perhaps it is time to settle. Indeed one needs to think about this at all stages, as there is always the risk of taking just one more step leading to just one further step and then an additional one and not knowing when to stop. How often one hears: "I have come all this way already and I am not going to stop now without going one step further."

One factor that has to be considered constantly is that of the cost of court proceedings. If a case reaches court then the usual rule is that the party losing the case has to pay the legal expenses of both parties. This can be an enormous figure if the matter has been going on for any length of time. It clearly does not make sense to pursue a dispute that is of low value unless one is absolutely convinced of success from the outset. Another phrase that is frequently heard is: "but it is a matter of principle". Those principles can come mighty expensive if things go wrong. The expense factor is a strong restraint.

This brings us on to two different ways of trying to settle a dispute, neither of which involves a court hearing in front of a judge. Both are supposed to be cheaper and quicker. These are:

1. *Arbitration.* In this process, there is an arbitrator either appointed by agreement between the parties or, more likely, chosen by some independent person. The arbitrator has wide powers to listen to the parties and decide how he is going to conduct the arbitration. It is more informal than a court. This form of procedure is generally used when an agreement specifically provides that this is the manner in which any dispute will be settled. The parties to the agreement, knowing how expensive a court hearing, and more particularly a High Court hearing, can be, opt for the arbitration route. An arbitration is almost always binding on the parties to ensure finality although in rare cases there might be an appeal to the courts if something very seriously wrong is alleged to have taken place.

2. *Alternative Dispute Resolution – "ADR".* This is a rather different animal. It is a form of mediation. The idea is that a trained mediator tries to find common ground between warring parties. The mediator can see the parties separately, unlike arbitration, as well as seeing them together. The hope is to find enough common ground to enable the parties to settle their differences without the expense of a full court hearing. The procedure is not binding on the parties, and anyone can back out at any time if they consider that they are going nowhere. One can end up with ADR achieving nothing and having added to the expense rather than reduced it. At one time the advocates of ADR were predicting that it would dramatically reduce the number of disputes taken to court but this

has not proved to be the case. Although ADR has its place in the right circumstances, it also has its limitations.

There is an appeals procedure if someone is sufficiently dissatisfied with the result of a case. An appeal from both a County Court and a High Court decision is to the Court of Appeal. This, of course, will add greatly to the expense and is something not to be undertaken lightly. An appeal is usually heard in front of three Lords Justice of Appeal, who may make a decision unanimously or by a majority. A majority decision might encourage the losing party to take his case to a second appeal, this time to the House of Lords which is the highest court in the land, and from which there is no further appeal. This final hearing will be before a number of Law Lords, typically five of them. The Law Lords are the most senior judges. At the time of writing, there is a debate as to whether to change the system and call the judicial branch of the House of Lords something else, such as the Supreme Court, and put them in a different location. There is bound to be a debate about whether this is a good or bad idea, but whether or not any change takes place, one thing will not change, namely, the expense of pursuing a case to the bitter end. One needs a mighty deep pocket even to contemplate taking a case all the way to the House of Lords.

When a case has been decided, what remedies does a court have?

1. *Damages*. As we have seen, the most frequent remedy is an award of money.
2. *Injunction*. Courts can order people not to do things. If a woman is being harassed, she may be able to obtain an injunction ordering the offender to stop. An injunction is not always to stop something

happening. Sometimes it can be positive, for instance, ordering documents to be handed over. If an injunction is needed urgently, judges can and do grant them to operate at once as a temporary measure, to be confirmed at a more formal hearing. There have been instances of High Court judges being phoned at home. An example of the need for speed is if there is a genuine fear of the publication of something that is legally covered by confidentiality. The Royal Family has used this route to prevent publication of confidential material by a former servant.

3. *Specific Performance.* This, as we have seen in contract, is a power to order the performance of an agreement to the letter, where damages are not considered an adequate remedy.

4. *A Lien.* This is the right of a creditor who is in possession of goods belonging to his debtor to hang on to them until he is paid his debt. The court does not make an order as such, but can confirm the creditor's right. An example is the right of a solicitor to keep a client's papers until that client has paid his bill.

5. *Prison.* This is not a remedy in the sense that it settles a dispute. It is a solution of last resort for civil matters. Although we do not have debtors' prisons any more, it is still possible to be sent to prison for non-payment, although it is extremely rare. Prison can also be the remedy for contempt of court. Courts take the flouting of their authority most seriously. An apology from an offender may be adequate, but if someone refuses to "purge their contempt" they may land up in prison. An overnight stay usually does the trick. Judges are slow to commit people to prison for contempt, but the power is there.

A question frequently asked is whether there is a limit to when a court action can be started. The answer is yes, and this is governed by the Limitation Act. Broadly, most actions have to be started no more than six years after the cause of action arises. For an action involving a personal injury claim, the action must be started within three years rather than six. The reason is a good one, namely that it is considered to be against public policy for this to be open ended. Whilst it is right that a person should have a decent length of time to make a decision, there must come a point when it is too late. It would be unreasonable for a possible defendant to be at risk of being sued for the rest of his or her life. Consequently, the Limitation Act is there to hold a balance, although there is no limitation period for serious criminal offences.

When does the period of three or six years start? Usually, this is obvious. If injury is caused in a road traffic accident, then the period starts at the time of the accident. If, however, there is some latent defect, then time runs from when the defect was discovered or ought reasonably to have been discovered. So, if a house is built with defective foundations but this only becomes apparent some years later, then time runs from the discovery of the defect and not from when the house was built. In one case, a property was converted into flats and a defect was discovered. Remedial work was carried out quite properly but failed to solve the problem because it did not get to the root of the problem which was insufficient damp proofing. A claim was made and the developers argued that it was now more than six years since the original work and therefore too late. The Court of Appeal decided that time ran from when the developers tried unsuccessfully to remedy the defect and so the claim was not "statute barred", that is, too late. The case could continue. (Alderson v Beetham organization 2 April 2003.)

The Limitation Act only applies to the starting of a court action. It does not regulate the speed with which an action proceeds once commenced. The courts are keen to try to ensure that cases are conducted without undue delay. There are time limits for various stages and, whilst failing to adhere to these limits will not always be fatal to a case, courts take a dim view of litigants who do not keep to them.

There is a general equitable rule about delay which was developed by the court of Equity. This is called the doctrine of laches, not lychees as one law student thought. He had obviously been out to a Chinese restaurant the night before! A person is not to be allowed to benefit by virtue of unreasonable delay. If there has been excessive delay, a court can order an action to be struck out for want of prosecution. So, just as there is not unlimited time to start an action, the same applies also to getting on with that action.

Another power that the court has is to declare a person a vexatious litigant. It is a power sparingly used. There are some people who catch an addiction to litigation and start case after case for the most trivial reasons. This can be most upsetting to their targets. If this gets out of hand, the court can be asked to declare the person a vexatious litigant. This does not mean that he is prohibited from starting another action since, like the boy who cried wolf, the next occasion may be genuine. However, he is not permitted to start a further case without the prior consent of the court. This is a strong disincentive and in practice usually does the trick.

19

LEGAL AID

The principle behind legal aid is to give the poorer sections of the community access to the law, which they would not otherwise be able to afford. There are two main criteria. The first is eligibility on financial grounds. All applicants have to declare their means. The very poor will be assessed with a nil contribution so they will not have to pay anything themselves. Others will be assessed with a contribution which will vary according to their means. They will be required to pay this contribution towards the costs incurred. It is not therefore a case of paying all or nothing.

The second criterion is the merits of the case. Both criteria are now decided by the Legal Services Commission with an appeals procedure if they refuse to grant legal aid. The Commission comes under the overall umbrella of the Department for Constitutional Affairs.

It is not always easy to determine whether the merits of the case deserve a grant, and there have been some high profile instances where commentators and the media have argued that legal aid should never have been approved. The cases of some, though by no means all, asylum seekers are an example. The intention is that a legally aided person should be put in the same position as someone who is funding his own case. He should be neither better nor worse off. The question should be whether a privately funded client of average means would be advised to proceed in the same circumstances. If the answer is no, then a legal aid certificate should not be granted.

Frequently, a limited certificate will be granted. Perhaps it will go no further than authorising the obtaining of counsel's opinion on the chances of success where there is a genuine doubt. Alternatively, even if there appears to be a very good case there may still be a limitation only to go to the point where the statements of case have been exchanged and before a court hearing. The matter then has to be reconsidered in order to see if it ought to be taken further and the certificate extended.

It is also the duty of the solicitor handling the case to keep in mind whether a case is proceeding as hoped or is going wrong. After all this is essential when dealing with a paying client and it should be no different in legal aid matters. So, if something crops up that may undermine the case, this should be reported to the legal aid authorities even if there is a valid certificate in force.

Legal aid is only available for certain types of work. A defamation action, for example, cannot be funded through legal aid. Many firms of solicitors find legally aided work unprofitable because the rates allowed are low compared with other work. This is particularly so in many parts of London because of the high overheads of running a business in the capital city, but this problem is not confined to London.

The above is aimed at civil work but legal aid is essential also in criminal matters. If an individual is accused of a serious crime, justice requires that there is proper legal representation and this has to be publicly funded if the accused is of limited means.

The legal profession has recognised that legal aid is not comprehensive and leaves what is called "unmet need". Many lawyers therefore carry out some work for little or no remuneration. Sometimes this will be done by firms who have agreed to take part in such initiatives but often, young lawyers will be permitted by their employers to spend time advising at law centres. This helps to plug a gap although there is, naturally, a limit to this sort of initiative. The Law Society, in particular, supports the idea. You may recall from the chapter on jargon that this goes under the title of "*pro bono*" work.

20

SOLICITORS AND BARRISTERS

There are two branches of the legal profession, solicitors, and barristers or "counsel" as they are referred to. There are far more solicitors than barristers who practise law. Broadly, solicitors are in direct contact with the public and there are few even quite small towns, let alone large ones, that have no solicitors practising in them. Firms of solicitors can be found in practically every high street and it is usually possible to see a solicitor at quite short notice or sometimes instantly if a problem is particularly urgent. London, particularly central London and the City, tends to be different as there is less passing business and many of the larger commercial transactions are conducted there. Certain of the largest City firms have what is practically a twenty-four hour service. One sometimes wonders whether they have a state of alert that matches or even surpasses the Ministry of Defence!

Barristers, on the other hand, usually come into contact with the public through solicitors and some other professionals such as patent agents. Barristers are instructed on particular points of specialism or matters that may end up in court. They tend to practise only in the major centres of population, with a very large concentration in London. Some people make the distinction between solicitors as general practitioners and barristers as specialists, although many, perhaps most, solicitors specialise to a greater or lesser extent. The public comes across solicitors far more frequently than barristers. As from July 2004, it has been possible, in most instances, for barristers to be instructed directly by the public. How this will develop remains to be seen.

Barristers at a senior level can be appointed to become Queen's Counsel (QC) or to "take silk" as it is called. The reason for this is that QCs are entitled to wear robes made of silk, as opposed to junior barristers whose gowns are made of wool. QCs are also called "Leading Counsel" and tend to take on the heavier cases and charge accordingly. It is the Lord Chancellor that has appointed QCs and this has been a slightly mysterious process with the old boy/girl network not being entirely absent. As this is being written, a debate is going on about the future of this system. It has been possible in more recent times for solicitors to become QCs.

In some countries, judges are a different profession but in the UK they are appointed exclusively from the ranks of barristers and solicitors; mostly barristers. Someone who wants to become a judge, particularly a senior one, is likely to start by qualifying as a barrister. Judges, even High Court judges, do not earn as much as the most successful barristers. There is considerable prestige in being appointed to the High Court bench and a knighthood comes with it but if a barrister has been used to a particular level of earnings, he/she might think twice before accepting an appointment. Appeal Court judges are nearly always appointed by way of promotion from the High Court bench, but it is possible to go straight from barrister to the Court of Appeal.

The very rigid divisions that used to exist between the two branches of the profession have loosened somewhat in recent years. It is now easier than it was to change from one branch to the other. Subject to certain fairly rigid conditions, it is now possible for solicitors to appear

in the High Court which previously was completely for-
bidden. In the County Court and in Magistrates' Courts,
solicitors have always been able to appear or had "the
right of audience" as it is termed. The training of both
branches now has more in common than used to be the
case. The terminology remains different. A solicitor is
"admitted" to the roll of solicitors on qualification,
whereas a barrister is "called to the bar". A budding
solicitor after exams has to enter into a training contract
with another solicitor (formerly called articles of clerkship) whilst for a potential barrister, the word is "pupillage". The full title of a solicitor is "Solicitor of the
Supreme Court". For a barrister the full name is
"Barrister-at-Law".

Solicitors are controlled by the Law Society, based in
Chancery Lane, London. Every solicitor, if he or she
wishes to practise, has to have an annual practising
certificate. Before this is granted he needs an accountant's
certificate if any client monies have been handled, and
certain training called Continuing Professional Development has to be undertaken. There is therefore an annual
check on all practising solicitors. Barristers are controlled
by the Bar Council and they also need to do further
training. Barristers must be a member of one of the four
"Inns of Court". These are Inner Temple, Middle Temple,
Lincoln's Inn and Gray's Inn all originating from their
geographical location in and around Holborn, just west of
the City of London. One of the odd quirks in becoming a
barrister is the need to eat a certain number of dinners in
the hall of the Inn of which he/she wishes to become a
member. This does help to create a spirit of camaraderie
and so is not as odd as it might at first sight appear. If you
want to be a member of what might be termed a sort of
club, then it is not unreasonable that you join in the
activities of that club.

I will conclude this chapter on a subject that has been

the source of much debate, namely whether there should be a unified profession, as there is, for instance, in Canada. Is there a need for two separate professions? An argument against is that, at the moment, all barristers are available to anyone who can afford their fees. In a unified profession, there is a fear that specialists in particular fields would be snapped up by the largest and richest firms of solicitors and their expertise would cease to be available to all. There might also be more difficulty in appointing judges. A converse argument is that a unified profession might help to cut costs as there is some duplication when a barrister is involved. Cutting out certain restrictive practices is the way things have been going and there is a lot to be said for this approach. One such practice that has gone is the rule that when a QC was appointed in a matter another junior counsel had to act as well. This is often desirable but it is no longer absolutely obligatory. Incidentally "junior" counsel is any barrister who is not a QC. There are some very senior "junior" barristers!

21

LAWS OF FOREIGN COUNTRIES

Until recently most would have said that the laws of foreign countries did not affect them. This is somewhat less so today. We may have a few shares in a company registered abroad or work abroad for a period. We may want to buy a holiday home or a timeshare in the Dordogne, Tuscany, Florida or one of the Spanish Costas. We may simply have a foreign holiday and come up against foreign law.

There is the well-known phrase "when in Rome do as the Romans" and this certainly applies to the law of another country when we are there. We have to obey the law wherever we go and, if we do not like the laws of a particular country, we have to accept this, or alternatively not go. This does not generally pose a problem as long as we do not carry out any provocative activities. Where people have come unstuck is in not appreciating the severity of some legal systems. Drug smuggling into some countries carries a life prison sentence or even the death penalty. There have been some high profile cases where foreigners have been caught out drug smuggling, giving rise to diplomatic incidents and involving governments. In many countries, handing out what either is or might be considered propaganda can land one in much trouble.

For most of us, the worst that is likely to happen is to

be involved in a traffic accident or to find oneself having a minor row with a local person. Common sense will tell you to avoid a confrontation especially if you cannot speak the language. Even in our closest neighbour, France, it is possible to be fined on the spot by the police. If one is alleged to have fallen foul of some minor motoring regulation it is better to pay a fine and continue one's journey. Technically it is a deposit to cover any fine that might be levied by a court but in practice no part of the deposit is likely to be refunded. When a French policeman is fingering your passport and your destination that evening is 200 miles away in Switzerland you do not argue!

How does one deal with matters that cross international boundaries? This is rather different.

This subject has two names. One is "private international law". The other is "conflict of law" reflecting the fact that two different legal systems may conflict when trying to decide an issue. Take an example. A contract is entered into between an English and a United States company to ship goods from the US to England in a Bermudan registered ship. The ship is due to call at a Spanish port en route but nearly sinks just off the Spanish coast. A Dutch salvage vessel is employed and the ship is eventually brought into the Spanish port. The law of which country is to apply to sort out all claims? The rule is that one has to look for what is called the "proper law" of the contract. This simply means the law most closely connected with the contract. Sometimes the answer is fairly obvious but in other circumstances it is not. There are then potentially two disputes to settle, firstly which country's law is to apply and secondly then to apply the law of that country to the contract.

I can hear someone ask if it would not be better for the parties to agree which law is to apply as a part of the contract. That is precisely what does happen in the majority of cases. It is quite common to find in holiday brochures and holiday insurance policies that one of the conditions is that the law of England is to apply.

It is not always possible to nominate which law is to apply. For instance, land and buildings are always subject to the law of the country in which the land and/or buildings are situated. This is known by yet another Latin phrase namely "*lex situs*", the law of the place or site of the land. This is clearly sensible since it would not be possible to insist on another country's law to apply. The practical effect of this is that your Spanish retreat is governed by Spanish law whether you like it or not. This in turn means that Spanish succession laws apply if you die owning the house. As we have seen, this is different from English law and you cannot leave the whole of the Spanish house to whoever you want. There are ways round this but it is an example of conflict of law.

Another vexed subject can be the enforcement of foreign judgments in the UK and vice versa. Generally, UK courts will recognise foreign courts and enforce their judgments and we in the UK expect foreign courts to uphold judgments of UK courts. It is more difficult, and problems arise, when the judgment was made by a court in a country with what we would regard as an oppressive regime.

A UK court will not enforce the tax laws of a foreign country. If someone comes here owing tax to another country, that will not be enforced here and the same is true in reverse. If someone leaves the UK owing tax, assets left here can be seized but he will not be followed to a foreign country and assets outside the UK will not be taken. However, the person concerned will not be able to return to the UK without risk. This is one of the tests of an independent country and so if we ever reached the point where an EU country could follow someone to another member country to recover arrears of tax, it would put a question mark on the true independence of the countries of the Union.

Tax matters between states are governed by what are called double taxation agreements. These are negotiated between states and the idea is to prevent income arising in one country and received by someone in the other country paying tax twice on the same income. These agreements are all bilateral, that is between two countries, but they tend to have a certain similarity to them. At its simplest, tax deducted in the paying country is allowed as a credit in the receiving country.

Two other topics that deserve a mention are tax havens and timeshares. Tax havens affect relatively few people but are important to the very rich. The principle is to move assets to a place where they will be shielded from the worst rigours of tax. As a general rule, the higher tax rates go, the more taxpayers look for tax havens to deposit their assets or even go to the extent of leaving the high tax country for good. For those living in the UK, the Channel Islands and the Isle of Man spring to mind as tax havens. Others are well known such as Monaco, a favourite of well paid sportsmen. There are less well-known ones such as the Cayman Islands, Netherlands Antilles and Liechtenstein.

There have been plenty of horror stories about time-share properties and the hard sell techniques used by sellers. A timeshare is quite unlike owning a property. What is owned is merely the right to use the property for specified periods each year. Other people have the right to use the same property at other times. There is nothing intrinsically wrong with a timeshare if it is properly organised. After a number of scandals, the Timeshare Act 1992 was passed, which gave some protection to purchasers. In particular there is a cooling off period with purchasers being given notice of the right to cancel.

The act only applies if the contract is subject to the laws of the UK and/or one of the parties to the contract is in the UK when the contract is entered into. Although this has largely dealt with abuses in the UK, it has not dealt with timeshares outside the UK when holidaymakers are collared whilst on holiday. This is an example of the limit to which UK law can go to protect its citizens in respect of assets abroad.

22

INTERNATIONAL LAW

The previous chapter dealt with what is called conflict of law or private international law. This chapter tackles what is sometimes called public international law. It covers such matters as treaties, mineral rights under the seas, war crimes and the role of the United Nations, matters with which the ordinary citizen is not directly involved but which may nevertheless affect him deeply. The most obvious example of such an effect is the declaring of war by one state on another. How much is it governed by an accepted body of law and how much by pure politics? This is not always an easy question to answer.

One has to say that the phrase "might is right" has been correct through most of history where tribes and then countries are concerned. The formation of empires throughout history is largely about the wielding of power and might. The Romans did not ask the people of Gaul and Britain if they could invade, neither did Alexander the Great or Hitler have a discussion with the leaders of the countries they sought to conquer. Empires come and go, but the process is governed by power (and some luck) and not by anything written down in the form of international law.

It is beyond the scope of this book to enter into a discussion about empires but some sort of force is usually required to create one, even if it then continues for a period by general consent. The power of the Royal Navy was an important factor in the success of the British Empire. Whether the European Union is seen by some as an attempt to create an empire without force would be a good subject for debate.

Some matters do have a basis that is covered by international law. How far do territorial waters extend and where do the high seas begin? There may be different limits for different purposes such as customs and fishing. There are international rules regarding who owns the mineral rights under the seas. With the ever increasing search for resources, this is likely to remain important. Basically, each country's boundaries are extended out into the sea. Countries with a long coastline such as the UK tend to do rather well out of this. The UK and Norway have been the two main beneficiaries of North Sea oil because of this.

A second area where the rules have been developed quite recently in historical terms is that of war crimes. The trial of the Nazi leaders at Nuremberg after the end of the Second World War set the ground rules. There had not been anything quite like it before. War criminals can now be brought to justice. Those accused will sometimes claim that it is the victor's justice brought for reasons of revenge. However, war crimes trials usually allege such heinous actions that, if they are proved, no right thinking person could consider that the perpetrators do not deserve punishment.

Agreements between individuals are called contracts. Between countries they will be given a title such as an accord or a protocol. The more important ones will be called treaties. These are binding agreements negotiated between the countries involved and then ratified by the respective governments. We have already had reference to the Treaty of Rome which set up what was originally called the European Economic Community or The Common Market, for short. It is now known as the European

Union. Two other particularly well-known treaties are the Treaty of Utrecht and the Treaty of Versailles. It was under the Treaty of Utrecht that Gibraltar was ceded to the United Kingdom in perpetuity.

The Treaty of Versailles was entered into in 1919 in the aftermath of the First World War. It carved up Europe and ordered Germany to pay vast war reparations. Some people say that in it were the seeds of the Second World War. This does bring us on to the subject of the international community trying to prevent damaging wars. In other words, was there some way of trying to blunt the "might is right" way of thinking?

After the trauma of the First World War, the League of Nations was formed. This was an organisation based in Geneva formed by the nations of the world to try to find a way of settling disputes peacefully. It failed in its endeavours and the Second World War is witness to that failure. There were a number of reasons for this but a very significant one was the inability of the League to enforce any of its decisions. Immediately after the Second World War in Europe was over and even before the war in the Far East had ended, the United Nations was formed and the charter was signed in San Francisco on the 26th June 1945. It started with enormous hope, following less than forty years in which the nations of the world had twice inflicted unimaginable suffering on each other. The preamble to the charter sets out the ideals and the charter itself puts in place the mechanism to achieve those ideals. It is worth quoting from the preamble:

"WE THE PEOPLES OF THE UNITED NATIONS DETERMINED
to save succeeding generations from the scourge of war, which twice in our lifetime has brought untold sorrow to mankind, and

to reaffirm faith in fundamental human rights, in the dignity and worth of the human person, in the equal rights of men and women and of nations large and small, and

to establish conditions under which justice and respect for the obligations arising from treaties and other sources of international law can be maintained, and

to promote social progress and better standards of life in larger freedom,

AND FOR THESE ENDS
to practice tolerance and live together in peace with one another as good neighbours, and

to unite our strength to maintain international peace and security, and

to ensure, by the acceptance of principles and the institution of methods, that armed force shall not be used, save in the common interest, and

to employ international machinery for the promotion of the economic and social advancement of all peoples,

HAVE RESOLVED TO COMBINE OUR EFFORTS TO ACCOMPLISH THESE AIMS."

The architects of the UN were determined not to repeat the mistakes of the League of Nations and so they created two principal bodies, the General Assembly and the Security Council. All member countries have a place on the General Assembly and one vote on every resolution. The

Security Council has just sixteen members. There are five permanent members, China, Russia (formerly the USSR), the UK, the USA and France plus other non-permanent members, elected for a two year term by the General Assembly. There were originally only six non-permanent members but the number was increased.

The Security Council has power by article 42 of the charter to sanction force to settle a dispute and all member states are supposed to make available armed forces, assistance and facilities in order to maintain international peace and security. The five permanent members of the Security Council have a veto on all resolutions, a power that is not used lightly. Article 2(7) prohibits the UN intervening in the domestic matters of members, and countries that do not like what the UN is proposing for them have frequently tried to maintain that Article 2(7) applies.

The Chief Executive is the Secretary General. It is not an easy post to fill because it needs someone who commands respect and is not thought to be in the pocket of any nation, particularly the larger and more influential ones. The first two, Trygve Lie and Dag Hammarskjold, were both Scandinavian – Norwegian and Swedish respectively. Trygve Lie called it the "most impossible job on this earth". Under Article 99 the Secretary General may bring to the attention of the Security Council any matter which in his opinion may threaten the maintenance of international peace and security. Quite a responsibility!

The UN has had a part to play in most international conflicts since the end of the Second World War. The Korean War was one of the earliest. It can send either observers or a peacekeeping force to any part of the world. In our own continent of Europe, the Balkans and Cyprus spring to mind. The ending of the Cold War has not lessened the need for UN intervention. Indeed the need for the UN seems to have increased due to more instability in certain parts of the world.

The UN has been the scene for high drama and tension for instance during the Cuban missile crisis in 1962 when nuclear war seemed a possibility. It has also been the forum for farce as on the occasion when the Russian leader Nikita Kruschev took one of his shoes off and banged it on the table in front of him.

How will the UN fare in the future? Your guess is as good as mine but it is the best we have got at the moment and has survived various crises. Funding it continues to be a problem with a number of countries not being very good about paying their dues on time. The United States has not always been the quickest of payers. However, the organisation is unlikely to fail through lack of money and we must remain optimistic about its future.

23

TRENDS

Crystal ball gazing tends to be a mug's game. It is almost impossible to predict the future, and most people who try to do so get it wrong. One can identify a number of trends that have taken place over the last thirty or so years and it is interesting to speculate on whether they will continue, or whether they have run their course.

1. *Consumer protection.* Legislation has helped to modify the old *caveat emptor* or buyer beware principle. This has included such areas as more rights for consumers, outlawing of unfair terms and the introduction of cooling off periods. It has also included the formation of the Financial Services Authority (FSA) which regulates the way in which financial services are sold to the public and who is permitted to market such services. There is no doubt that a body like the FSA was overdue with a number of unscrupulous people selling all sorts of unsuitable plans and schemes to vulnerable people. There have been a number of scandals. One instance is the selling of endowment mortgages to people for whom they were not appropriate. This trend may well have further to go.
2. *Anti discrimination protection.* This is not new if one includes the position of women as we have

seen earlier. Women were harshly treated until well into the twentieth century but, in more recent times, we have seen further legislation to prevent discrimination on the grounds of sex. In particular, there should be no favouring of men when filling job vacancies and a woman must not be offered less money merely on the grounds of her sex. Although seen as a measure to improve the lot of women, it should be noted that it applies equally to men and a man can bring an action if he thinks there has been discrimination against him purely because of gender. This might be alleged if, for instance, a business was started and run entirely by women, and men were never taken on even though ideally qualified. There are also the anti race discrimination provisions. This has now been followed by laws to stop discrimination in the workplace on the grounds of sexual orientation such as being homosexual or lesbian. It is now an offence to discriminate in the workplace on the grounds of religion. There can be a fine line between anti discrimination laws and the right of free speech; that is the ability of people to say what they believe, even if others strongly disagree. This is likely to be the cause of further debate.

People with disabilities are also given protection by the law. The most visible example of this, in public places, is the provision of ramps for people in wheelchairs.

3.   *Constitutional change*. There have been recent changes to the House of Lords by the cutting down dramatically of the number of hereditary peers who have the right to vote. Further changes to the House of Lords are promised and the phasing out completely of the right of hereditary peers to vote in the House is one proposal. The question would then be

whether we have a wholly appointed second chamber or one which is either entirely or partially elected. Changes are also likely to take place in the way the House of Lords as the final appeal court operates. The position of the Lord Chancellor has changed. Will his office be abolished altogether? We now have separate parliaments or assemblies for Scotland and Wales. There have been suggestions that there should be assemblies for the different regions of England. Questions need to be asked about this such as what it would do to the cohesion of England as a country and would it matter if only some regions had assemblies?

4. *Europe*. The EU is an issue that will not go away. How much power is to be retained at Westminster and how much are the EU institutions to have power over us? This is a matter that ultimately cannot be dodged or sidetracked. People have a variety of views from one end of the spectrum to the other but what has not yet been fully answered is the ultimate goal of the EU. Is there an ultimate goal or is it a question of seeing how it develops without a particular plan? How should this be decided and by whom? Many politicians have been bruised by the EU question but the issue is not magically going to disappear in a puff of smoke.

5. *Information technology*. The revolution in IT means that more information is available to everyone than in any previous era. This has its effect in many areas of our lives and the law is not immune. Will we all have access to sources of law so that there will be more DIY? Perhaps we will be able, at some point, to deal with many of our legal problems at the local supermarket after buying the groceries. Having lawyers available in chain stores to advise is something that may not be all that far away.

Law has always been subject to change and that is not going to alter. Sometimes the pace has been slow, followed by rapid and extensive changes. It is arguable that the law should not change too quickly. It should not change to fit in with a trend that passes as quickly as it arrives. We also need a degree of certainty and stability and this is one reason why judges do follow previous decisions in the majority of cases. This does bring us back full circle to the first chapter on the origin of law. The purpose is to regulate our behaviour so that the weak do not go to the wall and the strong suffer restrictions on their behaviour, to protect others.

GLOSSARY

Acts of Parliament Laws passed through both Houses of Parliament with the Royal Assent.

Anton Piller order A court order to search premises and take away papers before they can be destroyed.

Averaging Rule that if one is underinsured, one will only recover a proportion of any claim and not the whole of the loss.

Bar Council The organisation that governs the barristers' profession.

Bill A draft Act of Parliament which remains a bill until it has received the Royal Assent.

Blackstone, Sir William Well known eighteenth century lawyer.

Caveat Emptor Latin phrase meaning let the buyer beware.

Codicil A document amending a will.

Codified Law Whole body of law of a country written down as one code.

Common Law The old customs of the law of England and Wales.

Conflict of Law	How laws of different countries interact with each other.
Consideration	Value that has to be given in a contract.
Constructive Dismissal	Conduct by an employer making it impossible for an employee to stay on, leading to that employee claiming damages when he/she gives notice.
Court of Chancery	The court that administered the rules of equity.
Curia Regis	Latin for the King's Court set up by William I.
Denning, Lord	Senior judge in the latter part of the twentieth century well known for making robust decisions.
Distinguish-ing	A technique used by judges to highlight differences from a previous case so that they do not have to follow a previous inconvenient decision.
Equity	Rules of fairness introduced to get round rigidities of the common law.
Espinasse	A law reporter with a very poor reputation for accuracy.
Habeas Corpus	Latin for "produce the body". A remedy for people unlawfully imprisoned.
Hansard	Official report of all the proceedings in Parliament.
High Court	The court based in the Strand, London that deals with the larger cases. The Court of Appeal is also based there.
Injunction	An order of the court either to do or not to do something.

Inns of Court	Inner Temple, Middle Temple, Lincoln's Inn and Gray's Inn, one of which all barristers must join.
Invitation to treat	An invitation to make an offer leading to a contract.
John Doe	A fictional character invented by lawyers to help start a case.
Joint Tenancy	A type of joint ownership of property where the whole of the property passes automatically to the survivor on the death of one of the owners.
Judicial Review	The review of decisions of government and other decision making bodies by the court.
Jurisprudence	Theories of law and the philosophy behind laws.
Justinian	Roman Emperor who codified Roman law.
Laches	Equitable doctrine that a person should not gain an unfair advantage because of his delay.
Law Society	The organisation based in Chancery Lane, London, which governs the solicitors' profession.
League of Nations	Organisation set up after the First World War. A precursor to the United Nations.
Lex Situs	The law of the country where land or property is situated.
Lien	The right to retain someone else's property in certain circumstances.
Liquidator	Person appointed to wind up an insolvent company.

Lord Chancellor	Head of the judiciary and speaker of the House of Lords.
Magna Carta	The Great Charter agreed between King John and the Barons in 1215 giving certain basic rights to citizens.
Mareva injunction	An injunction to freeze assets if, for instance, it is suspected that they are about to be taken out of the jurisdiction of the courts.
Mens Rea	Latin for the necessary state of mind needed by someone who is accused of a crime.
Nisi	Latin for "unless", as in "decree nisi" where the decree will become absolute for a divorce "unless" there is an objection.
Obiter Dicta	Parts of a judgment that are persuasive but not essential to the decision.
Per Incuriam	Case decided without taking account of a relevant earlier decision and therefore not reliable.
Personalty	Broadly property that is not land or buildings.
Power of Attorney	A document by which one person authorises one or more other people to look after his or her affairs.
Precedent	The following of earlier decisions of the court.
Pro Bono work	Work done for no remuneration.
Probate	The court approval of the will of a deceased person.

Pupillage	Practical training of a barrister after the passing of exams.
Quantum	The amount at issue in a case as opposed to whether there is any liability in the first place.
Queen's counsel (QC)	Senior barrister or solicitor, mostly barristers, who tend to take on the more weighty cases.
Ratio Decidendi	The core reason(s) for a decision of the court.
Realty	Land and buildings.
Richard Roe	Like John Doe, a fictional character.
Rule of Law	Concept that everyone is subject to the same basic fair law.
Separation of Powers	Concept of spreading power between the government, Parliament and the judges.
Solon	Ancient Greek law maker.
Specific Performance	An order of the court to carry out something that has been agreed but not yet carried out.
Statute	An Act of Parliament, see above.
Statute barred	A cause of action that cannot be pursued through the courts because it happened too long ago and is barred by the Limitation Act.
Statutory Instruments	Delegated law made by a minister or some other authority under powers granted by an Act of Parliament.

Tenancy in common	A type of joint ownership of property where each owner can give away his share and it does not automatically pass wholly to the survivor on the death of the first.
Tort	A civil as opposed to a criminal wrong, for example, negligence.
Trust	An arrangement where property is managed by trustees for one or more other people.
Trustee in bankruptcy	Person appointed to manage the finances of someone declared bankrupt.
Uberrimae Fidei	Latin for utmost good faith, important in insurance.
United Nations	Successor to the League of Nations and based in New York.
Volenti non fit injuria	More Latin that means that if one volunteers to put oneself in a dangerous position one cannot bring an action if something goes wrong.
Will	Document setting out how property is to be divided up on death and appointing who is going to carry out the winding up.

INDEX

A

Acts of Parliament, 16–17, 18, 21–25, 40, 45, 53,152
Adverse occupation, 85
Alternative Dispute Resolution (ADR), 125–126
Anti-discrimination protection, 148–149
Anton Piller order, 30, 152
Appeals, 19, 126
Arbitration, 125
Articles of clerkship, 135
Assault, 64–65
Audience, right of, 134
Averaging, 77, 152

B

Bar, called to the, 135
    Council, 135, 152
Barrister-at-Law, 135
Barristers, 17, 133–136
Bill, 22–23, 152
Blackstone, Sir William, 15, 152

C

Care and control, 96
Case law, 16–20
Caveat emptor, 75–76, 152
Certiorari, 44
Chancery, Court of, 30, 153
Charities, 113–114
Civil law, 61
Close of pleadings, 124
Codicil, 116, 152
Codified law, 152

Commercial law, 104–109
Common law, 14–15, 152
Company law, 104–109
Concurrent sentence, 68
Conflict of law, 138, 152
Consecutive sentence, 68
Consideration, 71, 153
Constitution, written, 39
Constructive dismissal, 79–80, 153
Consumer protection, 76, 148
Contempt of court, 127
Contract law, 70–80
Contracts of employment, 79–80
Contributory negligence, 91
Copyright, 120–121
Counsel, 17, 133
    , Junior, 136
    , Leading, 134
County Courts, 16, 122, 126
Court of Appeal, 18, 19, 122, 126, 153
Criminal courts, 122–123
    law, 61, 63–69
Crown Court, 64, 123
Curia Regis, 28, 50, 153
Custody, 96

D

Damages, 73, 90, 126
Decree absolute, 95
    nisi, 95
Deeming, 54
Defamation, 86–87, 123, 131
Defence, 124

Delegated legislation, 24
Devolution, 46–47
Dicta, 19
Disclosure, 124
"Distinguishing", 19, 153
Divorce, 93
Duty of care, 87–88

E
Enduring power of attorney, 111
Equity, 29–31, 153
Espinasse, 16, 153
European Union, 25–27, 150
Ex parte, 50

F
Fact, questions of, 17
Family law, 93–99
Four year rule, 103
Freehold property, 81–82

H
Habeas Corpus, 36, 43, 153
Hansard, 23, 153
High Court, 12, 16, 18, 19, 122, 126, 153
    judges, 41
House of Commons, 22
        Lords, 18, 19, 22, 122, 126, 149–150
Human Rights Act 1998, 33–34

I
In camera, 50
Injunction, 30, 91, 126–127
Inns of Court, 135
Insurance, 76–78, 154
Intent, criminal, 64–65
International law, public, 142–147
Invitation to treat, 70–71, 154

J
John Doe, 53–54, 154
Joint tenancy, 85, 154
Judges, 16–18, 20, 23, 68, 134
Judicial Review, 20, 43–44, 154
    Separation, 96
Juries, 63, 64, 123
Jurisprudence, 35, 154
Justinian, 12, 154

K
King's Court, 28

L
Laches, doctrine of, 129, 154
Land law, 81–85
    , sale of, 56
Law, question of, 17
    reports, 16
    Society, 135, 154
Leasehold property, 82
Legal aid, 130–132
    fictions, 53–54
    Services Commission, 130
Legislation, 21–24
Lex situs, 139, 154
Libel, 86–87, 121
Lien, 127, 154
Limitation Act, 128–129
Limited liability companies, 104
Listed buildings, 102
Lord Chancellor, 30, 41, 155, 134

M
Magistrates, 63, 64
Magna Carta, 28–29, 50, 155
Malice aforethought, 65
Mandamus, 44
Mandatory orders, 44
Manslaughter, 65
Mareva injunction, 30–31, 155
Mens Rea, 64, 155
Misrepresentation, 72–73
Monarchy, 47–48
Murder, 65

N
Natural justice, 44
Negligence, 14, 87
Nisi, 155
Nuisance, 86

O
Obiter Dicta, 19, 50, 155

P
Parliament, 21–24, 40, 44–46
Partnership, 105
Passing off, 120
Patents, 118–119

Per incuriam, 19, 155
Personal injury claim, 128
Personalty, 81, 155
Plagiarism, 121
Planning law, 100–103
Pleadings, 124
Pollock, Sir Frederick, 15
Power of attorney, 111–112, 155
Precedent, 18, 155
Private companies, 105
    international law, 138
    members' bills, 22–23
Privilege, 87
Pro bono, 50, 132, 155
Probate, 116–117, 155
Prohibiting orders, 44
Prohibition, 44
Proper law of the contract, 138
Property Act, Law of, 32
    , managing, 110–117
Public limited companies, 105
Pupillage, 135, 156

Q
Quashing orders, 44
Quantum, 91, 156
Queen's Counsel (QC), 134, 156

R
Ratio Decidendi, 19, 50, 156
Realty, 81, 156
Redundancy, 79
Reform Act, 31
Remoteness of damage, 89
Richard Roe, 53, 156
Robbery, 68
Royal Assent, 22, 40
Royalties, 121
Rule of Law, 41–42, 156

S
Sale of Goods Act, 76
Scottish law, 50–51
Security of tenure, 83
Sentencing, 68
Separation of powers, 40, 156
Silk, take, 134

Slander, 86–87
Small Claims Courts, 122
Solicitor of the Supreme Court, 135
Solicitors, 17, 133–136
Solon, 12, 156
Specific performance, 30, 73, 74,
    127, 156
Statements of case, 124
Statute, 15, 156
    barred, 128
Statutory instruments, 24–25, 156
Stipendiary magistrates, 64
Summons, 123

T
Tax laws, 139, 140
Tenancy agreement, 82
    in common, 85, 157
    , joint, 85
Theft, 67–68
Timeshares, 140
Tort, 86–92, 157
Trade marks, 119–120
Treaties, 143
Tree preservation orders, 103
Trespass, 86
Trust, 112–113, 157
Trustee Act, 32, 113
    in bankruptcy, 107, 157

U
Uberrimae Fidei, 77–78, 157
Unfair Contract Terms Act 1977, 76
    Dismissal, 79
United Nations, 144–147, 157

V
Vexatious litigant, 129
Void marriages, 95
Voidable marriages, 96
Volenti non fit injuria, 91, 157

W
Wardship, 97
Wills, 59, 114–117, 157
    , living, 114
Writ, 124